Endorsements

"Lynn began praying with me in my garage twenty-five years ago. Out of that passion began a depth of sweet and never-ending intimacy. *Whispers of His Word* is an invitation for you to journey into the heart of God in ways you never dreamed possible. Those who do great things for God always begin with having deep relationship with God. Set your heart on pilgrimage and seize the day by daily listening to His heartbeat."

Lou Engle
Co-Founder and President, The Call
Author, *Digging the Wells of Revival* and *The Call of the Elijah Revolution*

"Twenty-five years ago Lynn was involved with us and started the young adult ministry. She wondered how to really listen and hear God. This book is the heart of that journey. As you begin to encounter the Lord through *Whispers of His Word* you will hunger for more of Him, for deeper revelation and greater depth in your relationship with the Trinity. This book will inspire and equip you for growing intimacy as you disciple nations in the midst of the coming worldwide harvest."

Che Ahn
Senior Pastor, H Rock Church
Founder and President, Harvest International Ministry
Author, *When Heaven Comes Down* and *Say Good-bye to Powerless Christianity*

"The crying need in all humanity—from CEO's to the newest kid starting at a fast food joint; from the penthouse, to the street person—is to have an ongoing, conversational relationship with God. Prayer is simply 'talking to God about the things you and he are working on together.' Conversation implies a mutual exchange which includes both talking and listening. *Whispers of His Word* shows us how to do both in relationship with God."

Todd Hunter
Anglican Bishop, Former National Director - Alpha USA
Author, *Giving Church Another Chance*

"Lynn Strietzel provides an easy on ramp to grow in the deep message of the Word through a practical but involving devotional style book. I enjoyed having such a simple but rich tool to lead me through thought provoking questions that engaged not only my mind but my spirit. *Whispers of His Word* truly will connect you to God's voice and thoughts over your life."

Shawn Bolz
Senior Pastor, Expression58
Author, *Keys to Heaven's Economy* and *The Throne Room Company*

"Any service for the Lord can get stymied when we leave relationship with Jesus aside because of our focus on goals, projects, and Kingdom work. Anything, no matter how good, that does not also lead one into deeper relationship with Jesus must be suspect! I have seen a singular passion in Lynn Strietzel's life through my friendship with her over this past decade....a heart after the heart of God and hearing what He has for her at any moment of any day. *Whispers of His Word* reflects this and its pages ooze an invitation to be lost in the wonder of partnership with the Living God....to always take time to deepen that most important Relationship of all relationships, intimacy with Jesus."

Bryan Thompson
Founder and Director, story4all
All Nations, 12 years, Operation Mobilization, 4 years, Youth With A Mission, 16 years

"Lynn Strietzel is one of the most joyous, hopeful and courageous women I know. She has ripened, grown rich and strong under the pressures of many years of missionary challenges. *Whispers of His Word* invites the readers to encounter for themselves the never-failing source of enduring and sustaining joy, shutting out deafening and disappointing voices and sharpening our senses to hear the whispers of God."

Dierk Mueller
Pastor, Kraftwerk Evangelical Free Church
Director, Bibelschule Dresden, Germany

"Lynn's deep passion for intimacy with the Lord is rivaled only by her desire to welcome others into that secret place with Him. *Whispers of His Word* will help usher you into that quiet place where you see, hear and know the Savior for yourself."

Rich Schmidt
Pastor, Christian Missionary Alliance, 16 years

"Lynn visited us in Brazil and taught our children how to be sensitive to the voice of the Lord. Not only did she impact their lives, but my own in stirring up the desire for a deeper intimacy with the Lord and more sensitivity to His voice. Over the years I have seen the Lord use Lynn to impact people all around the world. God is knocking at the door of our hearts and just waiting for us to allow Him to banquet with us! *Whispers of His Word* will teach you how to tune your heart to His on a daily basis. You will experience that deeper, sweeter communion you desire to have!"

Jeff Hrubik
President, Project AmaZon
Overseerer 500 churches in Brazil

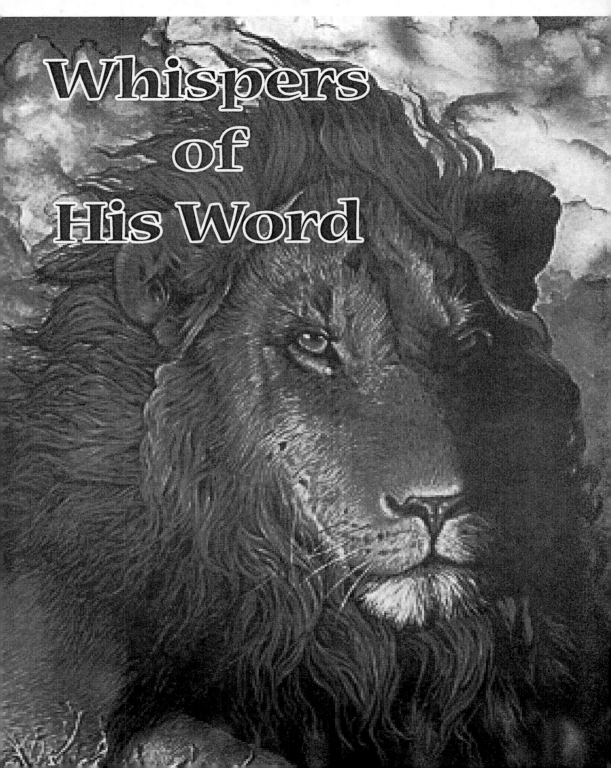

"As the great harvest of souls begins, *Whispers of His Word* is a wonderful tool to equip individuals to fall in love with Jesus and His Word. This book creates an excitement to pray and encounter the Lord in the beauty of holiness. The section on the Holy Spirit and the book of Acts will shape church history. Lynn's book is wonderful for people who have loved the Lord all their lives and, it is wonderful for individuals who just met the Lord."

Anne Kalvestrand
Overseer, Missions Training, Bethel Church
Instructor, Bethel School of Supernatural Ministry
Director, The Art of Peace Institute
Author, *Establishing Healing Rooms: Stewarding the Anointing of John Alexander Dowie*

"Lynn is an amazing gift to the Kingdom, a great friend and loved deeply among her friends. She is a person full of passion and commitment to the nations. Not only does she declare that message but also has lived it! *Whispers of His Word* is a great book and easy read. Her style makes her book a great devotional and leaves you with more intimacy with the Lord. I recommend this book to all my friends."

Wendell McGowan
Senior Leader and Itinerant Ministry, River City Church
Author, *Firewalker* and *The Unfolding*

"The great gift of Pentecost is the return of Joel's Spirit of prophecy that is for "all flesh." This means that anyone who has the indwelling and empowering Spirit can carry on two-way conversations with God. What we need is a practical tool to help us get started and *Whispers of His Word* is just the ticket. The first time I used it I heard the Lord speak clearly and powerfully, and I believe that you can too! "

Bill Jackson
Adjunct Professor, St. Stephen's University
Author, *Quest for the Radical Middle: A History of the Vineyard*
And *Nothings Gonna Stop It: The Storyline of the Bible*

"Lynn Strietzel is a women in love with Jesus and His Word. Lynn waits on the Lord combining a deep hunger for both the written Word and those sweet personal encounters with the living Jesus that take your breath away. Whispers of His Word will help to lead any hungry soul into those precious moments of intimacy with our Lord Jesus Christ."

John Sturges
Revival Pastor, Bethel School of Supernatural Ministry
Conservative Baptist and Christian Missionary Alliance Pastor for 35 years

"Obedience to the Father sharpens our hearing so that we can listen to God well. Lynn has consistently demonstrated her willingness to obey God over many years and seasons of her life. I believe this has brought about intimacy in her relationship with the Lord. I recommend *Whispers of His Word* because it aptly describes Lynn's personal journey as I have known her over many years."

Peter Lau
Overseer, Living Waters Hong Kong, 2000-2010
Overseer, Aichina: A Children's Ministry in Hong Kong

"The Lord created us for an eternal love relationship with Himself, and in that relationship He longs to saturate us with all that He is. That's how we're meant to live – full of God Himself. And when we are full, everything we do becomes the "overflow of the everflow" of His redeeming love. *Whispers of His Word* provides a simple but profound opportunity for those who long to step into that fullness to take a few moments every day to encounter afresh the One who has invited us into an ongoing dialogue with Himself. And once we begin to listen, we will be hooked, for we'll never hear a sweeter, more comforting voice…anywhere!"

Dr. Myra Perrine
Church Resource Ministries
Adjunct Professor, Simpson University andTozer Theological Seminary
Author "What's Your God Language"

"Lynn Strietzel is a friend and a mother in the faith to me. The integrity of her journey with the Lord makes her trustworthy to invite many others to come alongside. *Whispers of His Word* commissions us to ask God the deepest, most poignant questions of our soul, inviting an encounter with the Living God. No journey is more essential than allowing the Spirit of Christ to search and know us and to remove every barrier to our fully receiving His love. It is in this place of intimacy where revolutionaries and earth-shakers become all they are meant to be."

Wendy Andrews
Pastoral Leadership team, Kansas City Boiler Room
Former National Co-leader, 24-7 Prayer USA and Campus America

"Knowing what God is speaking today is crucial for everyone who wants to enter into the fullness of his heavenly inheritance and union with God. I doubt that there's a single person alive – inside and outside the church walls - who wouldn't like to know which words are being formed today by the same lips that spoke light and life into existence. Yet only few truly understand that hearing very often requires an active act called: "listening".

Throughout history there have been those who devoted their entire lives 24/7 to seek God's face. Today we face the challenge with busy schedules to find the place of heavenly rest and the wells of living water. Lynn Strietzel has been learning and teaching about this topic for over 25 years and the Lord has been and is now more than ever using her to activate the body of Christ to a new norm of listening. *Whispers of His Word* doesn't only inspire for abstract deeper realms, but provides a practical day to day approach that helps even the busiest person to discern His voice!"

Daniel Vogler
Youth Evangelist & Artist, Germany
Founder, Street Invasion Ministries

Foreword

Two characteristics of a believer which will ensure a closer walk with God are hunger and humility. They are the attributes of Jesus, who came to serve not to be served because He always wanted to do what He saw His Father doing.

When I first met Lynn Strietzel I saw these two attributes of humility and hunger in full measure. What I know now is that these attributes are the fruit of foundations in her life, foundations upon which all of life can be built. *Whispers of His Word* gives the reader the opportunity to build those foundations for themselves.

This devotional study will lead you not to answers in the word but to the Living Word, the marriage of the living indwelling Holy Spirit and the Word of God.

Recognizing the need to learn is in itself an act of humility and should for all of us be a life long journey. This simple yet effective book will engage you in that journey whether for the first or the umpteenth time. But I warn you, it may be the most intimate study guide you have encountered in a while. Intimate because you will be asking questions that may seem almost impertinent or risky to ask, but as with Moses you will be led boldly to ask the audacious like Moses when he asked, "Show me Your Glory."

Once our heart is positioned to learn, the art of asking questions is the expertise that the hungry ones exude. Jesus, of course the Master of asking questions, provokes His listeners to think for themselves, to discover their own answers and hence more questions. Jesus was leading the hearers to become hungry for themselves. Yet He who knew and had access to all, modeled the humility of asking His Father.

As Lynn guides us, the questions lead us to relationship. We discover more about ourselves, each other and Him and have yet even more questions. Hunger is not a one time deal in the kingdom it is the way of an ever expanding life in God. Jesus in the great Sermon on the Mount said, "Blessed are they who hunger and thirst after righteousness."

This truth is the journey of this Whispers of His Word. You will be blessed as you hunger and thirst. The goal is to not just know answers, not even just to know Him, although that would be treasure enough! The goal is to know ourselves in relation to Him and to understand how we are a part of His great plan for His kingdom here on earth.

I believe you will receive an impartation as you ask the questions which have been fashioned by a true lover of Jesus. They are the questions learned at the feet of Jesus, learned by one ministering in nations cut off from fellowship with much of the Body, but leaning always and daily into Him. They are the questions which she is freely giving to you, learned herself in a sacrificial life. Don't miss this impartation, pause long enough to ask yourself where these questions come from and you will find that they come from a heart not merely an intellect.

Whispers of His Word will nourish you, draw you in to Him but also send you out. The answers will demand of you that you become the living word and impact your world because of it!

Paul Manwaring
Global Legacy Overseer
Senior Management Team, Bethel Church, Redding, California

Acknowledgements

Mom and Dad, I love you dearly! Thank you for laying your life down for your 11 children. I honor you for your hunger for Jesus. Dad and Nan, thank you for your encouragement and support over the past seven years! Mom, as you're watching with that great cloud of witnesses, I honor you for living and loving well! My family, siblings and spouses, nieces and nephews, thank you. Your love for the Word and pursuit of our Lord inspires and encourages me. To my nieces and nephews, my longing is that I would leave a legacy for you and your children's children … that all I think, pray, say and do will thrust you into your destiny that Jesus would get His full reward from our family.

My family in the Body of Christ, I'm so grateful you have loved me, lifted me and carried me for the past 37 years as I've followed Jesus living in six countries. I'm grateful we share many precious living stones, faces of people, in our crown, our wedding gift to our Bridegroom. I would never have lived such a blessed life apart from you! **Bill and Beni, Kris and Kathy, Danny and Sheri, Paul and Sue, and my Bethel Church Family,** thank you for giving it all to co-labor with our Lord to see His kingdom, heaven on earth. It's an honor to walk with you! **Che Ahn and Lou Engle**, thank you to you and your families for giving yourself to the nations and the unborn. I'm so grateful to be filled with the Spirit and to have prayed with you for revival at six in the morning in your garage!

To my favorite teachers….children from **Lamb's Lunch, Anaheim Vineyard Christian School, Inland Vineyard, and North Langley Vineyard,** ex-heroin addicts in Hong Kong, and orphans in Taichung, thank you for imparting childlikeness to me, for learning together to live in adoption and to listen and obey our Shepherd! To some of my unsung heroes, **Jim, Lisa, Maria and Nicholas,** thank you for believing God is good in the midst of some of life's greatest challenges!

Elsie Fadner, thank you for telling me how to be born again and being a part of the beginning of my never-ending pilgrimage to know Him and see His face more clearly! **Peggy Filasky,** thank you for helping me know that I was special to both my Father and the Body of Christ. For loving my uniqueness even my inability to sing on key or clap on beat… but I really know that song! **Anne Kalvestrand,** you honor me every time I'm with you. I'm so grateful that you believe in me, sometimes more than I even do. You help me to experience more than I ever imagined and you inspire me to reach for the high calling of God that rests upon me! **Morgan, Shirley and Brad,** thank you for going the extra mile, rather the extra ten thousand, to publish this book!

Dear Dylan, 6/11

One thing I ask from the Lord,
this only do I seek:
that I may dwell in the house of
the LORD all the days of my life,
to gaze on the beauty of the LORD
and to seek him in his temple….
My heart says of you, "Seek his face!"
Your face, LORD, I will seek

Psalm 27: 4 and 8

May you hear Jesus
every day of your
life. And may you
seek His face more
than anything else! Lynn
Strietzel

Whispers of His Word

Encountering Jesus

By Lynn Strietzel

Published By
Accent Digital Publishing, Inc
2932 Churn Creek Rd.
Redding, CA 96002
(530) 223-0202

ISBN 978-1-60445-058-3
© 2010 Lynn Strietzel

Cover Picture - Ken Petrarnek
Painting Title: "Facing the Wind"
The theme of this painting is the apostolic & prophetic
embrace of the Kingdom of God that is emerging on
the horizon. The Hebrew word is "Ruach" which can be
interpreted wind, breath or spirit.
Kenpetranek@charter.net

Dedication

To John Wimber for introducing me to intimate worship I had never dreamed possible, for helping me to receive and walk in the favor of God, and for eyes of compassion to see the poor.

To Bill Johnson for catalyzing an unquenchable hunger and quest to see the incomprehensible beauty of the face of God, and for kingdom understanding how heaven invades earth, especially through an honoring love of others and powerful prayers.

You have both been life-changing gifts from God. I will forever be grateful to Him for bringing you into my life.

Most of all I dedicate not only this book, but once again I dedicate all of my life to **Jesus.** I love Your ways, I love Your face, I love Your Name, I love Your Presence. I love how You love me. You alone are worthy of worship. For all eternity I honor You above all else. I long to see the kingdoms of this earth become the kingdoms of our God and Christ. You and You alone deserve all the honor and all the glory for all eternity.

Lynn Strietzel

Contents

Introduction

A world waiting, not yet even hoping, but longing for the possibility of true love... God, the God Man, longing for them to hear His heartbeat...a handmaiden pregnant with prophetic purpose, yet unaware... a symphonic book waiting to bring all three together.

We don't hear someone's heart beat unless we lean on his or her breast. Like John the Apostle, this is our great privilege. This is our inheritance. The joy of our lives is to hear our Lover's heartbeat. The louder beat is His love for us. The softer beat is His love for others. The more we receive God's love, the more we can respond and love Him back. The more we receive God's love, the more we can love others like He loves them.

Welcome Pilgrim! Welcome to the adventure of exploring the height, depth, and breath of God's love. No exploration to the far reaches of the universe carries more magnificence. No exploration to the deepest ocean carries more adventure. No exploration of the strong force of one atom carries more anticipation. God has no limits. What if our 'ceiling' of intimacy today became the our floor of intimacy tomorrow? Welcome to this eternal and infinite journey. Let's go!

Lynn Strietzel

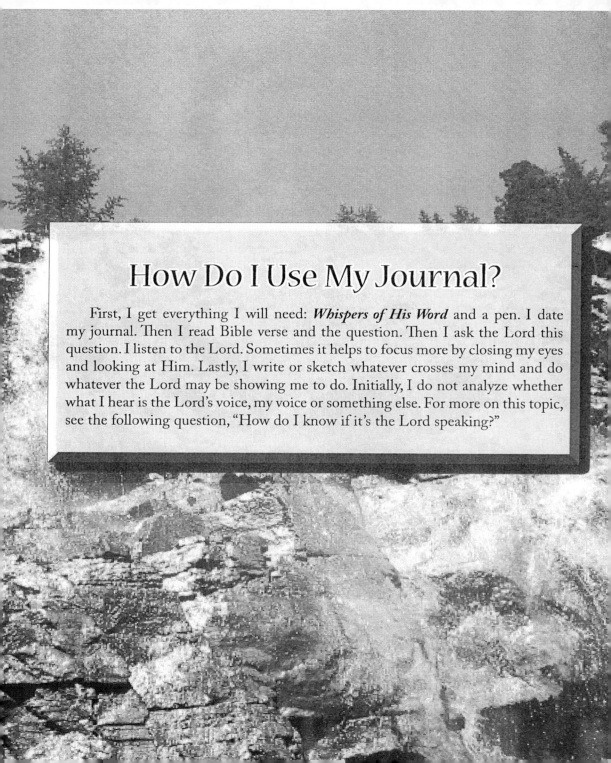

How Do I Use My Journal?

First, I get everything I will need: ***Whispers of His Word*** and a pen. I date my journal. Then I read Bible verse and the question. Then I ask the Lord this question. I listen to the Lord. Sometimes it helps to focus more by closing my eyes and looking at Him. Lastly, I write or sketch whatever crosses my mind and do whatever the Lord may be showing me to do. Initially, I do not analyze whether what I hear is the Lord's voice, my voice or something else. For more on this topic, see the following question, "How do I know if it's the Lord speaking?"

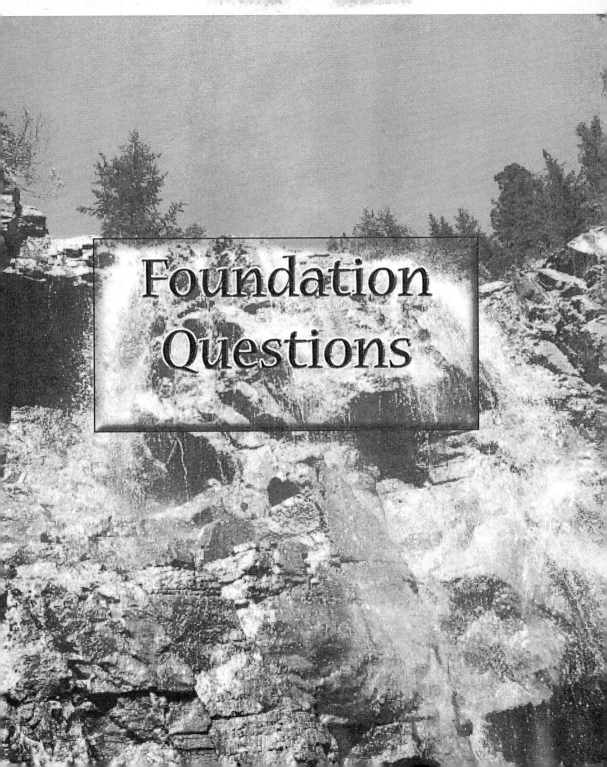

Foundation
Questions

How Do I Find Bible Verses?

A Bible reference is like an address. For example Psalm 27:4 is the address to one verse in the Bible. First find the Table of Contents on one of the very first pages of your Bible. Look for the name of that book. All 66 books of the Bible are listed by name. You look for "Psalm". Way over on the right of the name of the book is the page number where that books starts. Find that page in your Bible. If "Psalm" is page number 725, go to page 725. Find the chapter. The chapter is always the first number after the name of the book. Usually it is the largest and darkest number. If you want to find Psalm 27:4, then look for chapter 27. Then find the verse. Verses are always the second number and come after the colon : Usually they are the little numbers in our Bible. In Psalms 27:4 you want verse 4.

Why does God Speak?

God speaks because it is part of His nature. It is WHO He is. He is called the Word of God. He did not just "think" Creation. He spoke Creation because He is the speaking God. One of the common names for Jesus is Shepherd. Three times in John chapter ten, He says that His sheep hear His voice. We are created in His image, therefore our voice also has authority.

God speaks because He wants to do it again. "It" is anything He has already done and even more. According to Psalm 78:11, the Israelites wandered because they forgot. They forgot who God was. They forgot what God did. And they forgot who they were. They lost their identity. To help them remember, God commanded them in Deuteronomy chapter six, to tell their children the stories, the testimonies of who He is and what He has done. As the children heard the stories, they would have a hunger to see and hear God do it again. In Malachi chapter three, it talks of an eternal heavenly book, the Book of Remembrance, the record of people's conversations with God and about God.

God speaks because He wants to invade our world. John chapter one says, "In the beginning was the Word….and The Word became flesh." Jesus' very name is, "the Word" and He invaded earth by becoming a human being—now that's invasion! In Luke chapter 24, between Jesus appearing to the women and appearing to the apostles, Jesus takes time out to appear to two guys who were talking about Him. After He appeared they were so excited that they ran and told the apostles. While they were talking about Jesus the second time, Jesus showed up again and appeared to the apostles.

One of the greatest invasions of all time is recorded in Acts, the first two chapters. From the Resurrection to the Ascension, Jesus summarized all His teachings in the phrase "speaking pertaining the things of the kingdom." Jesus instruction to His disciples just before He ascended was to wait for the Holy Spirit who would give them power to be His witnesses. When the Spirit of Jesus came at the first Pentecost, He came with power—a roaring wind, flames of fire, and world-changing voices. That invasion changed all of history. People who did not believe in Jesus complained that Jesus' disciples had turned the world upside down. Our world is waiting for our voice—for us to turn the world right side up by the invasion of the kingdom on heaven on earth!

Who has God Spoken to?

Throughout Scripture Godly people heard God speaking. Genesis says that Adam & Eve walked and talked with God in the cool of the evening.

In Genesis chapter three, Enoch had a close friendship with God. In Genesis chapter six, Noah received instructions on how to build an ark and how to gather the animals. In Genesis chapter 11, Terah was told to move to Canaan, but he disobeyed and stopped part way.

In Genesis chapter 12, God told Abraham that he would be a blessing to all peoples. In chapters 15, 17, and 18 of Genesis, God spoke to Abraham again, and again, and again. God warned King Abimelech in a dream in Genesis chapter 20. In chapter 21 God spoke to Hagar in the desert. Then in chapter 22 God tells Abraham to kill Isaac. God spoke to Abraham's servant in Genesis chapter 24. Then God spoke to Isaac in chapter 26. He spoke through a dream to Jacob in Genesis chapter 28 and through an angel in chapter 32.

In Exodus chapter three, God spoke with Moses through a burning bush. Then in chapter 28 the Urim & Thummin was used to determine the will of God. Why did the priest carry them close to his heart? Maybe, because our hearts are where we hear God. Hearing God is essential in determining God's will.

Throughout the Bible, God spoke in many different ways. In Joshua, Judges, and the book of Samuel He spoke through dreams, a voice while sleeping, instructions through the prophets and so on. God spoke to David throughout the Psalms. In the books of the Bible, the prophets saw visions, heard words, had angels visit them. Habakkuk is actually a record of conversations with the Lord.

In John 5:30, Jesus said that He did nothing by Himself. He only did what He saw His Father doing. Throughout the Gospels we have glimpses of His incredibly intimate relationship and communication with His Father.

God has spoken clearly to many others throughout church history. To name just a few: Jonathan Edwards, Charles Finney, D.L. Moody, A.B. Simpson, James Frasier, Aimee Semple McPherson, Corrie Ten Boom, John G. Lake, Smith Wigglesworth, William Branham, Kathryn Kuhlman, T.L. Osborn, Billy Graham, Bill Bright, Joy Dawson, Jack Hayford, along with many little-known, yet great saints the Lord honors.

Why Can I Hear God?

The natural world that we live in…the world we see, is often a picture for us of the supernatural spiritual world we live in but cannot see. A picture for us in the natural is a baby. Do babies have ears when they're born? If you slammed a door would the baby hear this and maybe start to cry? The answer to these two questions is obviously, "Yes."

Right after a baby is born do they know who's talking to them? When people talk to a baby, does the baby know what the words mean? The answer to these two questions is also obvious, "No."

So, how do babies learn? Babies learn who is talking to them by hearing the same person many times. Babies learn the meaning of words by hearing lots of words over and over again.

In the spiritual world it works the same way. When we're born again spiritually we have spiritual ears. Right away our spiritual ears can actually hear God speaking to us. However, even after we are born again, we don't always know who is speaking. And when we're first born again, we don't fully understand the meaning of all God is saying.

So how do we learn? We learn the same way a baby in the natural learns. We learn to know who's speaking by hearing God speak to us many times. We also learn what it means by hearing lots of words.

Amazingly, we already have lots of words--the Bible. The Scripture is God speaking to us!!! The Bible is the foundation for all of our hearing God. We never hear God tell us something that's opposite or against what the Bible says, although we may hear things that are not specifically written in the Bible, for example seeing a picture of a bicycle. The Bible is always true and right. There were no mistakes in the original writing of the books of the Bible. Over the centuries people have tried to copy and translate them very accurately.

How Does God Speak to us?

God spoke to people in the Bible in many different ways. He still speaks to Christians today in these ways. Some common ways are seeing a photo or movie clip, seeing or hearing a word, sentence or song, hearing or remembering Scripture or an experience, having a dream or vision, smells, trembling, heat, weakness or fainting, angels visiting, and sometimes being taken somewhere. He is the Shepherd. He is the One speaking. We are simply His sheep, the ones who hear His voice. He can choose many ways to speak. Our desire is to be a disciple, a learner. Good learners are good listeners.

In I Kings 19:11-12, Elijah did not hear God in the thundering storm. He did not hear God in the earthquake. He did not hear God in the roaring fire. He heard God in the gentle whisper. Often when God speaks it is a whisper, a faint sound, a quick flash of sight, almost like something subliminal. God speaking in a whisper is easy to miss, to not even notice. We become better listeners as we practice intentional listening. It's almost like there is a TV channel where our Shepherd is speaking and we need to tune our eyes and ears to His voice.

It Seems That God Isn't Speaking. Why?

I don't know. Sometimes, I just really don't know. None of the reasons I mention here apply. I don't have an answer for why He doesn't speak right now. But here are a few things that I have found helpful.

First, sometimes it seems like God isn't speaking because I'm not really listening. I have not really quieted my own heart to actually listen. Often quieting my heart is the hardest part. Actually hearing God is the easy part. Imagine sitting in the living room with several people talking and the TV turned on. If someone in the bedroom is saying something, it is very hard to hear him or her. Maybe I just need to go into the bedroom with Jesus, close the door to all the other voices and then quietly listen. In the following section, "How Can I Listen to God?" There are some ideas on how to be quiet and listen.

Second, sometimes I ask God something but He doesn't answer. He simply reminds me that I have not yet obeyed the last thing He spoke to me. So if I listen and don't hear anything I ask Him if there is any sin or disobedience that is stopping me from hearing Him.

Third, sometimes people don't hear God speaking because they have a distorted view of Father God. They do not know that He is good all the time. Sometimes we believe that God is trying to get us to fail so He can punish us. Remember Adam and Eve. God gave them thousands of trees with fruit good to eat. He wanted them to have the best chance to succeed. Only one was forbidden. After they sinned they hid. Why did they hide? Why didn't they talk with God? Could it be they felt shame and fear at being naked and vulnerable? Do we sometimes fear being vulnerable and naked before God? Do we sometimes run away from His voice? I John says, "There is no fear in perfect love." God's love is perfect. Even in the midst of Adam and Eve's sin, God had already provided a covering. He had already killed an animal to use the skin to cover them--a picture of the Lamb of God slain since the beginning of the world. Are we sometimes afraid to hear God's voice because we are afraid He is mean? If a good dad is good to his kids, how much more is our Daddy in heaven good to us!

Fourth, sometimes people do not hear God because they really believe they cannot. Jesus Christ did so many miracles John says a world of books could not contain the record. Jesus had all authority. Jesus walked perfectly filled with the Holy Spirit. And yet, this Jesus could not do many miracles in Nazareth because of their unbelief. Sometimes people do not hear because of their unbelief. The truth, recorded in John chapter 10, is Jesus is the Shepherd and His sheep, you and I, hear His voice.

How Can I Listen To God?

Quieting my heart is the biggest key in listening to God. Therefore, find a quiet place and a specific time. Listening to God the same time and place every day usually works best. Have everything ready before you start to listen – Bible, *Whispers of His Word* and pen.

As you use, *Whispers of His Word*, write the date, read the question, read the Bible verse. Reading aloud sometimes helps to focus. Read the question again and listen. Blind people learn to listen really well because they can't see. Try closing your eyes. It may help you to listen and not be distracted.

Look at Jesus and listen. If you've asked Him to come into your heart and wash your sins away, He will never leave you. He's in your heart. Look at Him. I like to focus on His eyes. While you're looking at Him, ask Him the question.

If you feel distracted by thinking of something you need to do, just write it down. This may be something God is already speaking to you about. Then focus again on Jesus, and ask Him the question. Remember He is eager to talk with you.

How Do I Know What It Means?

It is important to see that the Scripture and the question are related. We need to know that what the Lord speaks to us relates to the Bible. Look up the Bible verse, even if you already memorized it. Ask the Lord what it means or if He wants to show you more details. To grasp the broader meaning, it helps to read the whole section around the verse. Sometimes reading the same verse in different versions of the Bible helps us understand it better. The translators use slightly different wording. If some words are confusing, look up the meaning of that word in a dictionary. There are many other Bible helps.

Sometimes it takes time to know what it means. Wait patiently. Keep asking God. Keep listening. Keep meditating on the verse. I often ask a friend, who knows more of the Bible, to help me understand my dream or something I heard.

Is It Really God Speaking?

The Bible is the basis for everything we hear. Ask people who disciple you to help you see how the words you heard relate to the whole Bible. If the things you heard aren't written about in the Bible that's fine. If the things you heard are opposite of what is written in the Bible, then listen to your disciplers and teachers as they correct parts of what you heard. It doesn't mean that we can't hear what the Lord is saying, it's just that we made a mistake. Everybody makes mistakes sometimes. Fear of making mistakes or fear of what others may think of us are some of the biggest hindrances to our walking out our destiny in the Lord. Our heavenly Father desires us to be like children…passionate risk-takers, courageous servants, worshipping priests and humble kings!

One time Michael, a 7-year old friend of mine thought God said, "I'm bad at spelling, too". Since the Bible says God knows everything, what he heard isn't true. We looked at some Bible verses together. Then he asked God, "God, since you're so good at spelling, how do you want to help me be a better speller?" We're all learners--that's what the word, "disciple" means, a learner. Nobody is perfect and it's good to always keep learning. This was a wonderful opportunity for my little friend to hear the Lord speak to him, even if it took a couple of tries.

How Do I Obey The Things I Heard?

God may have spoken many things to you. Most often He says things to us that are very personal and only for us. Things like how much He loves us and cares about the details of our lives. How He understands us, helps us, is with us, and will never leave us. It is good to thank Him for his love, His kindness, His goodness or whatever He is showing us about Himself. Also, it is very good to worship Him for whom He is and tell Him how awesome He is. When He reminds us of something special He did for us, we thank Him for the specific ways He has been loving, kind, and good to us.

Sometimes the Lord tells us that we are saying or doing things that are not good. When He says this we say, "I am sorry for saying _____. I know it was sin and I asked Jesus to forgive me. Now would you forgive me?"

Sometimes God tells us things about other people. Usually this is so we can pray for them. It is usually best to intercede for that person or those people right away. After interceding, we ask the Lord if He wants us to say anything to them, pray with them, or do anything for them.

Maybe the Lord is speaking to us about the lost in Taiwan, orphans in a war torn area, the poor without food in India. If it's a group of people and we don't know them, then we intercede for them. We ask Jesus if there is more we might do to help them.

Dear Dad

The Father Heart of God

What is your picture of a dad? Think about this. Is your picture someone who is gentle and kind? Will always help you and comfort you? Loves you no matter how many mistakes you make? Always has time for you? Understands you? Feels hurt when you feel hurt? Really likes you? Wants to be your best friend? Makes sure you get everything you need?

Your Father in heaven knows every little detail about you. He knows about your dreams and hopes. He knows what you like and don't like. His hands formed you before you were born. He sees every day of your life—the happy ones, the sad ones, every day that already happened… and all the days still waiting to happen. He understands when you feel sad, angry or afraid. He is always with you to help you. He chooses you to be His best friend. He loves you no matter how many mistakes you make. He will never leave you or even forget you. How could He forget you when He writes your name on the palm of His hand!

While answering the questions, experiment and use different names for Father: Dad, Daddy, Papa, Abba, etc. Choose the name that is most personal for you.

For you created my inmost being;
you knit me together in my mother's womb.
Psalm 139:13

1. Dad, You made me so wonderful. Why?

Date: ___/___/_____

THANK YOU

Where can I go from your Spirit?
Where can I flee from your presence?
Psalm 139:7

2. Abba Father, I will never be far from You. Why not?

Date: ___/___/_____

Even there your hand will guide me,
your right hand will hold me fast.
Psalm 139:10

3. Holy Spirit, You are my guide? What do You want me to do?

Date: ___/___/_____

_____
_____
_____
_____

The Lord appeared to us in the past, saying:
"I have loved you with an everlasting love;
I have drawn you with loving-kindness.
Jeremiah 31:3

4. Daddy, Your faithful love for me draws me closer to You. How?

Date: ___/___/_____

_____
_____
_____
_____

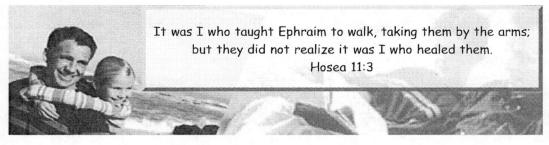

It was I who taught Ephraim to walk, taking them by the arms;
but they did not realize it was I who healed them.
Hosea 11:3

5. Papa, when I was a child, You taught me how to walk. How did You do that?

Date: ___/___/_____

_____

_____

_____

_____

I led them with cords of human kindness, with ties of love;
I lifted the yoke from their neck and bent down to feed them.
Hosea 11:4

6. Father, You lead me with Your kindness and love. Why?

Date: ___/___/_____

I LOVE YOU

7. Daddy, when I was a baby You bent down and fed me. Why?

Date: ___/___/_____

_____
_____
_____
_____

"The Lord your God is with you, He is mighty to save.
He will take great delight in you, he will quiet you with His love,
He will rejoice over you with singing."
Zephaniah 3:17

8. Dad, when do You sing over me?

Date: ___/___/_____

_____
_____
_____
_____

9. Father, You are incredibly delighted in me. Why? When?

Date: ___/___/_____

_____
_____
_____
_____

How great is the love the Father has lavished on us,
that we should be called children of God!
And that is what we are!
The reason the world does not know us is that it did not know him.
1st John 3:1

10. My heavenly Papa, I am Your child. How do You feel about me?

Date: ___/___/_____

_____
_____
_____
_____

This is how God showed his love among us:
He sent his one and only Son into the world
that we might live through him.
1st John 4:9

11. Daddy, You loved me first. Why first?

Date: ___/___/_____

_____
_____
_____
_____

This is love:
not that we loved God, but that he loved us
and sent his Son as an atoning sacrifice for our sins.
1st John 4:10

12. Father, You loved me so much You let Your Son die for me. Why?

Date: ___/___/_____

_____
_____
_____
_____

And so we know and rely on the love God has for us.
God is love. Whoever lives in love lives in God, and God in him.
1st John 4:16

13. Dad, You love me so much. How close of friends do You want us to be?

Date: ___/___/_____

_____
_____
_____
_____

There is no fear in love. But perfect love drives out fear,
because fear has to do with punishment.
The one who fears is not made perfect in love.
1st John 4:18

14. Father, sometimes I am afraid of letting You love me. Why?

Date: ___/___/_____

_____

_____

_____

_____

We love because he first loved us.
1st John 4:19

15. Papa, You loved me first. Who do You want me to love? How?

Date: ___/___/_____

_____

_____

_____

_____

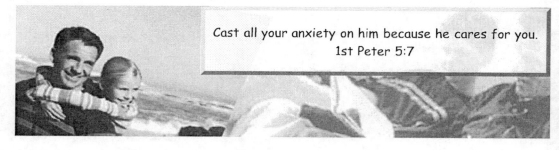

Cast all your anxiety on him because he cares for you.
1st Peter 5:7

16. Daddy, You care about every little thing in my life. Why?

Date: ___/___/_____

_____
_____
_____
_____

Keep me as the apple of your eye;
hide me in the shadow of your wings
Psalm 17:8

17. Dad, I am the apple of Your eye. Why am I so special to You?

Date: ___/___/_____

_____
_____
_____
_____

If we are faithless, he will remain faithful,
for he cannot disown himself.
2nd Timothy 2:13

18. Papa it says that, You always keep Your promises. Sometimes it seems like You don't. Why?

Date: ___/___/_____

_____

_____

_____

_____

The Sovereign Lord is my strength;
he makes my feet like the feet of a deer,
he enables me to go on the heights.
Habakkuk 3:19

19. Daddy, how do You help me to be strong?

Date: ___/___/_____

_____

_____

_____

_____

He tends his flock like a shepherd:
He gathers the lambs in his arms and carries
them close to his heart;
he gently leads those that have young.
Isaiah 40:11

20. Papa God, You hold me in Your arms. How? Why?

Date: ___/___/_____

_____
_____
_____
_____

Who has measured the waters in the hollow of his hand,
or with the breadth of his hand marked off the heavens?
Who has held the dust of the earth in a basket,
or weighed the mountains on the scales and the hills in a balance?
Isaiah 40:12

21. Father, You hold all the oceans in the palm of Your hand. What is that like?

Date: ___/___/_____

_____
_____
_____
_____

22. Dad, You measure the stars with Your fingers. How do you want to show Your largeness to me?

Date: ___/___/_____

_____

_____

_____

_____

> The Lord appeared to us in the past, saying:
> "I have loved you with an everlasting love;
> I have drawn you with loving-kindness.
> Jeremiah 31:3

23. You already love me, Daddy. But sometimes I try so hard to get You to love me more. Why?

Date: ___/___/_____

_____

_____

_____

_____

24. Papa, You already love me just the way I am. Why?

Date: ___/___/_____

_____

_____

_____

_____

For you did not receive a spirit that
makes you a slave again to fear,
but you received the Spirit of sonship.
And by him we cry, "Abba, Father."
Romans 8:15

25. You are my "Abba Father", my Dear Dad. Why did you adopt me?

Date: ___/___/_____

_____

_____

_____

_____

I have made you known to them,
and will continue to make you known
in order that the love you have
for me may be in them and that I
myself may be in them."
John 17:26

26. Daddy, You love Jesus so much. How can I love Jesus more?

Date: ___/___/_____

_____

_____

_____

_____

He restores my soul.
He guides me in paths of
righteousness for his name's sake.
Psalm 23:3

27. Father God, I want to bring honor to Your name today. How can I do this?

Date: ___/___/_____

_____

_____

_____

_____

Even though I walk through the valley of the shadow of death,
I will fear no evil, for you are with me;
your rod and your staff, they comfort me.
Psalm 23:4

28. Papa, You want to protect and comfort me. When I'm afraid, what should I do?

Date: ___/___/_____

_____

_____

_____

_____

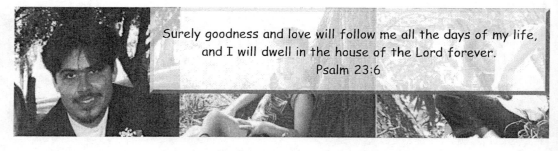

Surely goodness and love will follow me all the days of my life,
and I will dwell in the house of the Lord forever.
Psalm 23:6

29. Father, everyday You show Your goodness and faithful love to me. What about today?

Date: ___/___/_____

_____

_____

_____

_____

The Lord will fulfill his purpose for me;
your love, O Lord, endures forever-
do not abandon the works of your hands.
Psalm 138:8

30. Dad, You never leave me. Why not?

Date: ___/___/_____

_____

_____

_____

_____

God is so
Good!

We are Forgiven, Whole and Free

Jesus died on the cross for our sins. One day several children were discussing this. Suddenly, they all started crying. They had been mean to people, stolen things, lied, disobeyed, had a bad attitude, etc. Regardless of what kind of sin, they all began to feel deep sadness for their sin. They realized that they had hurt Jesus. They realized that they had committed a crime against the Creator of the Universe.

They asked Jesus to forgive them and to wash their hearts clean. They asked His Spirit to come inside them and help them not sin. They began to feel clean and pure inside. They knew that they were forgiven for their sin because Jesus died for them. They were so happy that they could hardly wait to share this joy with their family and friends.

Have you ever felt dirty or unclean? Regret or self-hatred? Rage or terror? Jesus paid the price for you personally to be completely pure and totally free. Just ask Jesus to wash you, forgive you and set you free.

"For God so loved the world that he gave his one and only Son, that whoever believes in him shall not perish but have eternal life.
John 3:16

1. Father God, You love me so much. Why this much?

Date: ___/___/_____

_____

_____

_____

_____

2. Abba Daddy, You want me to have eternal life. Why?

Date: ___/___/_____

_____

_____

_____

_____

For he chose us in him
before the creation of the world
to be holy and blameless in his sight.
Ephesians 1:4

3. Papa, You chose me before the world was made. How did You know me?

Date: ___/___/_____

_____
_____
_____
_____

In him we have redemption through his blood,
the forgiveness of sins,
in accordance with the riches of God's grace.
Ephesians 1:7

4. Father, what are the riches of Your grace to me?

Date: ___/___/_____

_____
_____
_____
_____

For we are God's workmanship,
created in Christ Jesus to do good works,
which God prepared in advance for us to do.
Ephesians 2:10

5. Father, what good things have You prepared for me to do?

Date: ___/___/_____

_____

_____

_____

_____

"... and the way of peace they do not know."
Romans 3:17

6. Dad, what is the way of peace? How can I live this?

Date: ___/___/_____

_____

_____

_____

_____

But now a righteousness from God,
apart from law, has been made known,
to which the Law and the Prophets testify.
Romans 3:21

7. Jesus, You promised to make me right in God's eyes. How will You do this?

Date: ___/___/_____

_____
_____
_____
_____

This righteousness from God comes through
faith in Jesus Christ to all who believe.
There is no difference,
Romans 3:22

8. Jesus, You died to take away my sins. When did I begin to trust that You died for MY sin?

Date: ___/___/_____

_____
_____
_____
_____

For all have sinned and fall short of the glory of God,
and are justified freely by his grace
through the redemption that came by Christ Jesus.
Romans 3:23-24

9. Father, You say I am not guilty. Why?

Date: ___/___/_____

_____

_____

_____

_____

God presented him as a sacrifice of atonement, through faith in his blood.
He did this to demonstrate his justice, because in his forebearance
he had left the sins committed beforehand unpunished--
Romans 3:25

10. Jesus, You died for everyone. Why did You die for me?

Date: ___/___/_____

_____

_____

_____

_____

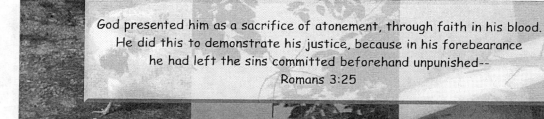

God presented him as a sacrifice of atonement, through faith in his blood.
He did this to demonstrate his justice, because in his forebearance
he had left the sins committed beforehand unpunished--
Romans 3:25

11. Daddy, there is no punishment for sin. Why not? How do want me to live?

Date: ___/___/_____

12. God, how am I right with You? When did I trust and become right with you?

Date: ___/___/_____

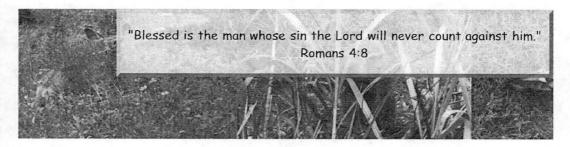

"Blessed is the man whose sin the Lord will never count against him."
Romans 4:8

13. Lord, You don't count sin against us. Why not? Why not my sin?

Date: ___/___/_____

Through whom we have gained access by faith
into this grace in which we now stand.
And we rejoice in the hope of the glory of God.
Romans 5:2

14. Christ, I want to stand with You in the place of grace. How can I?

Date: ___/___/_____

Not only so, but we also rejoice in our sufferings,
because we know that suffering produces perseverance;
perseverance, character; and character, hope.
Romans 5:3-4

15. God, what kind of character do you want me to have?

Date: ___/___/_____

_____
_____
_____
_____

And hope does not disappoint us,
because God has poured out his love into
our hearts by the Holy Spirit,
whom he has given us.
Romans 5:5

16. Holy Spirit, You fill my heart with hope and love. How?

Date: ___/___/_____

_____
_____
_____
_____

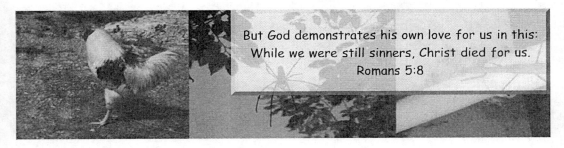

But God demonstrates his own love for us in this:
While we were still sinners, Christ died for us.
Romans 5:8

17. Father, You let Jesus die for me. Why me?

Date: ___/___/_____

_____
_____
_____
_____

Don't you know that when you offer yourselves to someone to obey him as slaves,
you are slaves to the one whom you obey--whether you are slaves to sin, which leads
to death, or to obedience, which leads to righteousness?
Romans 6:16

18. Jesus, what kind of a Master are you? What's most important to You?

Date: ___/___/_____

_____
_____
_____
_____

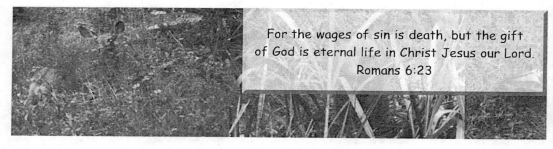

For the wages of sin is death, but the gift
of God is eternal life in Christ Jesus our Lord.
Romans 6:23

19. Dad, You gave me the free gift of eternal life. Why? Why me?

Date: ___/___/_____

_____
_____
_____
_____

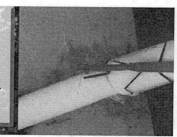

Those who live according to the sinful nature have
their minds set on what that nature desires;
but those who live in accordance with
the Spirit have their minds set on what the Spirit desires.
Romans 8:5

20. Holy Spirit, set my mind on You. What do You desire?

Date: ___/___/_____

_____
_____
_____
_____

You, however, are controlled not by the sinful nature but by the Spirit, if the Spirit of God lives in you. And if anyone does not have the Spirit of Christ, he does not belong to Christ.
Romans 8:9

21. Holy Spirit, I love You and surrender everything to You. How do You want to lead me?

Date: ___/___/_____

_____

_____

_____

_____

The Spirit... who is a deposit guaranteeing our inheritance until the redemption of those who are God's possession--to the praise of his glory.
Ephesians 1:14

22. Holy Spirit, You are a guarantee that God fulfills his promises. What has He promised to me?

Date: ___/___/_____

_____

_____

_____

_____

And by that will, we have been made holy through the sacrifice of the body of Jesus Christ once for all.
Hebrews 10:10

23. Father, how have I been made holy?

Date: ___/___/_____

_____

_____

_____

_____

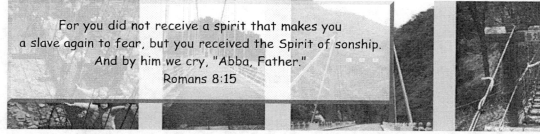

For you did not receive a spirit that makes you a slave again to fear, but you received the Spirit of sonship. And by him we cry, "Abba, Father."
Romans 8:15

24. Abba Father, how did I receive the Spirit of sonship? How is my life changed?

Date: ___/___/_____

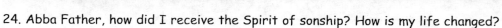

_____

_____

_____

_____

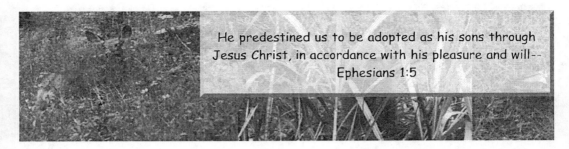

He predestined us to be adopted as his sons through Jesus Christ, in accordance with his pleasure and will--
Ephesians 1:5

25. Daddy, You are so happy to adopt me. What does "adopt" mean to You?

Date: ___/___/_____

_____

_____

_____

_____

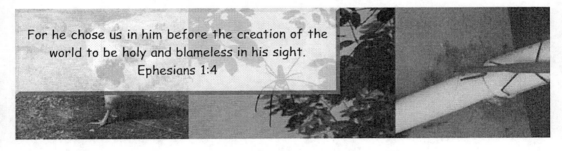

For he chose us in him before the creation of the world to be holy and blameless in his sight.
Ephesians 1:4

26. Father, You chose me to be in Jesus. How am I in Jesus?

Date: ___/___/_____

_____

_____

_____

_____

But you are a chosen people, a royal priesthood,
a holy nation, a people belonging to God,
that you may declare the praises of him who
called you out of darkness into his wonderful light.
1st Peter 2:9

27. Jesus, You called me out of darkness into light. How can I live in the light?

Date: ___/___/_____

28. King of Kings, how am I to live as a royal priest?

Date: ___/___/_____

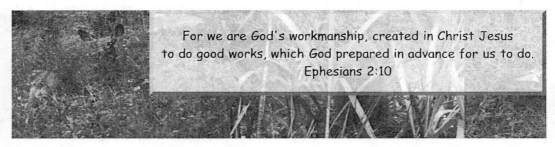

For we are God's workmanship, created in Christ Jesus
to do good works, which God prepared in advance for us to do.
Ephesians 2:10

29. God, I'm Your masterpiece—Your great work of art. What do I look like to you?

Date: ___/___/_____

_____

_____

_____

_____

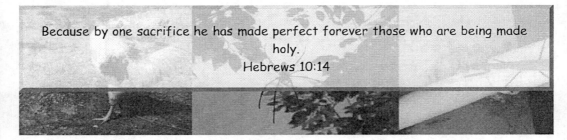

Because by one sacrifice he has made perfect forever those who are being made
holy.
Hebrews 10:14

30. Jesus, I'm made perfect and being made holy. How?

Date: ___/___/_____

_____

_____

_____

_____

*B*I*B*L*E

The Word Changes Lives

HOLY BIBLE

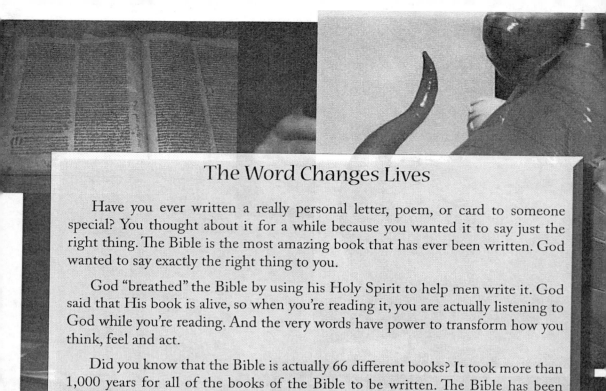

The Word Changes Lives

Have you ever written a really personal letter, poem, or card to someone special? You thought about it for a while because you wanted it to say just the right thing. The Bible is the most amazing book that has ever been written. God wanted to say exactly the right thing to you.

God "breathed" the Bible by using his Holy Spirit to help men write it. God said that His book is alive, so when you're reading it, you are actually listening to God while you're reading. And the very words have power to transform how you think, feel and act.

Did you know that the Bible is actually 66 different books? It took more than 1,000 years for all of the books of the Bible to be written. The Bible has been translated into more languages than any other book. It has also been read by more people than any other book. The Bible contains your history, your identity, and your destiny. Now that's a really special book! It is an awesome book—written specifically for you!

Jesus' disciples saw him do many other miraculous
signs besides the ones recorded in this book.
John 20:30

1. Jesus, the disciples didn't write ALL of your miraculous signs in the Bible. Why not?

Date: ___/___/_____

_____
_____
_____
_____

So the Word became human and lived here on earth among us.
He was full of unfailing love and faithfulness.
And we have seen his glory, the glory of the
only Son of the Father.
John 1:14

2. Jesus, You are the Word that became flesh. Why did You become flesh?

Date: ___/___/_____

_____
_____
_____
_____

Above all, you must understand that no prophecy in Scripture ever came from the prophets themselves or because they wanted to prophesy. It was the Holy Spirit who moved the prophets to speak from God.
2nd Peter 1:20-21

3. Holy Spirit, You helped and inspired men to write the Bible. How?

Date: ___/___/_____

_____

_____

_____

_____

All Scripture is inspired by God and is useful to teach us what is true and to make us realize what is wrong in our lives. It straightens us out and teaches us to do what is right.
2nd Timothy 3:16

4. Holy Spirit, You led people to write all of the Bible. Why all?

Date: ___/___/_____

_____

_____

_____

_____

All Scripture is inspired by God and is useful to teach us
what is true and to make us realize what is wrong in our lives.
It straightens us out and teaches us to do what is right
.It is God's way of preparing us in every way,
fully equipped for every good thing God wants us to do.
2nd Timothy 3:16-17

5. Teacher, what do You want to teach me?

Date: ___/___/_____

_____

_____

_____

_____

6. Jesus, how does the Bible train me to live right?

Date: ___/___/_____

_____

_____

_____

_____

For the word of God is full of living power.
It is sharper than the sharpest knife,
cutting deep into our innermost thoughts and desires.
It exposes us for what we really are.
Hebrews 4:12

7. Holy Spirit, the Bible is like a sharp knife. How does it help me?

Date: ___/___/_____

_____

_____

_____

_____

8. Spirit of God, my heart is Yours. What do You want to say to me?

Date: ___/___/_____

_____

_____

_____

_____

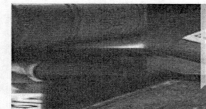

But they delight in doing everything the LORD wants;
day and night they think about his law.
Psalm 1:2

9. Daddy, what Bible verse do You want me to meditate on?

Date: ___/___/_____

10. Lord Jesus, meditating on the Bible is so important to You. Why?

Date: ___/___/_____

11. Holy Spirit, I want to dream at night about You and Your Word. How can I?

Date: ___/___/_____

The law of the LORD is perfect, reviving the soul.
The decrees of the LORD are trustworthy,
making wise the simple.
Psalm 19:7

12. Jesus, Your Word brings life to my soul. What do You want to say to me?

Date: ___/___/_____

_____

_____

_____

The commandments of the LORD are right,
bringing joy to the heart. The commands of
the LORD are clear, giving insight to life.
Psalm 19:8

13. Lord, You want Your commands to bring joy to my heart. How?

Date: ___/___/_____

_____

_____

_____

14. Christ, how are Your commands radiant giving light to my eyes?

Date: ___/___/_____

_____

_____

_____

They are more desirable than gold,
even the finest gold.
They are sweeter than honey,
even honey dripping from the comb.
Psalm 19:10

15. Jesus, Your Word is a treasure and it is sweet. How can I taste it more?

Date: ___/___/_____

_____
_____
_____
_____

They are a warning to those who hear them;
there is great reward for those who obey them.
Psalm 19:11

16. Abba Papa, if I obey Your Word there's a reward. What kind?

Date: ___/___/_____

_____
_____
_____
_____

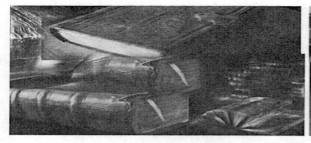

Happy are people of integrity,
who follow the law of the LORD.
Psalm 119:1

17. Lord Jesus, I want to follow Your law. I want to be blameless. How can I?

Date: ___/___/_____

_____

_____

_____

_____

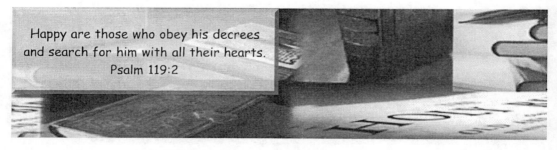

Happy are those who obey his decrees
and search for him with all their hearts.
Psalm 119:2

18. Jesus, how can I seek You with all my heart?

Date: ___/___/_____

_____

_____

_____

_____

You have charged us to keep your commandments carefully.
Psalm 119:4

19. Word of God, I want to faithfully keep Your commandments. Which one right now?

Date: ___/___/_____

_____

_____

_____

_____

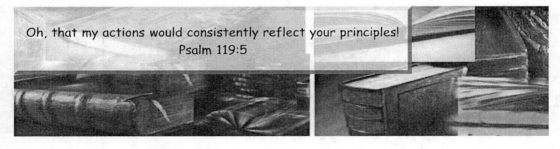

Oh, that my actions would consistently reflect your principles!
Psalm 119:5

20. Lord, how can my actions reflect your principles?

Date: ___/___/_____

_____

_____

_____

_____

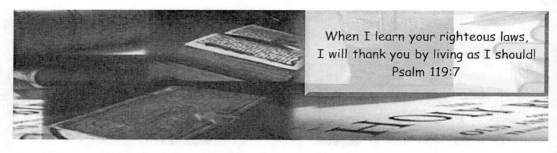

When I learn your righteous laws,
I will thank you by living as I should!
Psalm 119:7

21. Papa, how can I live like You want me to live?

Date: ___/___/_____

_____

_____

_____

_____

How can a young person stay pure?
By obeying your word and following its rules.
Psalm 119:9

22. Jesus, how can I stay pure?

Date: ___/___/_____

_____

_____

_____

_____

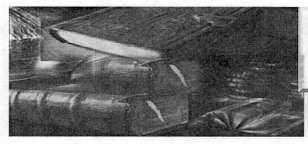

I have hidden your word in my heart,
that I might not sin against you.
Psalm 119:11

23. Spirit of God, You want me to hide Your Word in my heart. How can I?

Date: ___/___/_____

_____
_____
_____
_____

I have recited aloud all the laws you have given us.
Psalm 119:13

24. Lord, You want me to say your Word aloud. Why aloud?

Date: ___/___/_____

_____
_____
_____
_____

Do not snatch your word of truth from me,
for my only hope is in your laws.
Psalm 119:43

25. Jesus, why is my only hope in Your Word?

Date: ___/___/_____

_____

_____

_____

_____

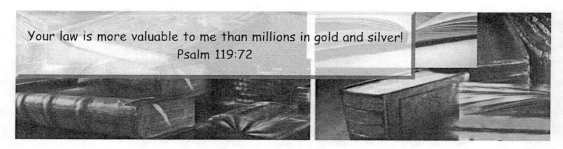

Your law is more valuable to me than millions in gold and silver!
Psalm 119:72

26. Jesus, how valuable is the Bible to me?

Date: ___/___/_____

_____

_____

_____

_____

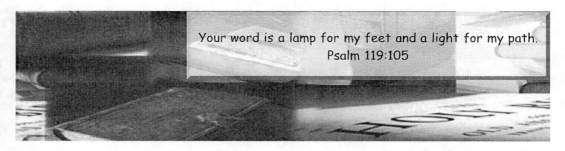

Your word is a lamp for my feet and a light for my path.
Psalm 119:105

27. Father, Your word is a light to show me where to walk. Where do You want me to walk?

Date: ___/___/_____

_____

_____

_____

_____

Beautiful girls and fine young men will grow faint and weary, thirsting for the LORD's word.
Amos 8:13

28. Living Word, how can I be more hungry and thirsty for Your Word?

Date: ___/___/_____

_____

_____

_____

_____

And the people of Berea were more open-minded than those in Thessalonica, and they listened eagerly to Paul's message. They searched the Scriptures day after day to check up on Paul and Silas, to see if they were really teaching the truth.
Acts 17:11

29. Jesus, Word of God, I want to study the Bible. I want to see if what people say is true. How do You want to help me?

Date: ___/___/_____

30. Holy Spirit, why is it good to search the Scripture everyday?

Date: ___/___/_____

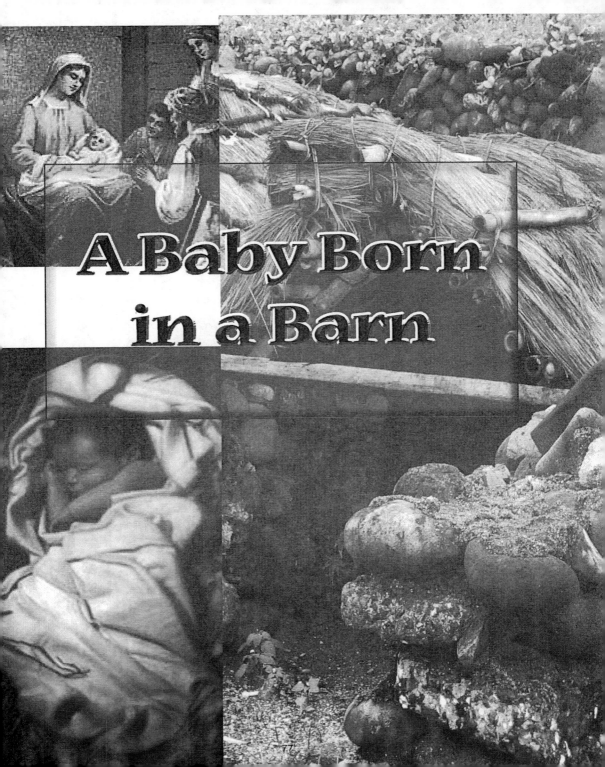

A Baby Born in a Barn

The Christmas Story

What's your favorite day of the year? Some people's favorite day is their birthday. Your birthday is special because you are special. On Christmas we celebrate Jesus' birthday. It's special because Jesus is so special. Jesus is God. Before Jesus was born He lived in heaven with His Father. He also lived with angels—lots of them! He created them. He created the universe; the sun, all the stars, the planets, the oceans, the continents, plants and animals. Best of all, He created us!

But we committed a crime against God, the Creator of the Universe. We sinned. We couldn't go to be with Jesus in heaven. So Jesus left heaven. He was born on earth so He could die for us. That's why Jesus' birthday is so special to celebrate. We remember how very much He loves us.

On Christmas we celebrate Jesus' birthday. Sometimes people give birthday presents. Ask Jesus what gift He would like on His birthday. The Bible says that we give to Jesus when we give to someone in need. This Christmas we could give Jesus a birthday gift by giving to someone in need. Do you know someone who needs help? Food? Clothes? Do you know someone who needs encouragement? Comfort? Prayer? Healing?

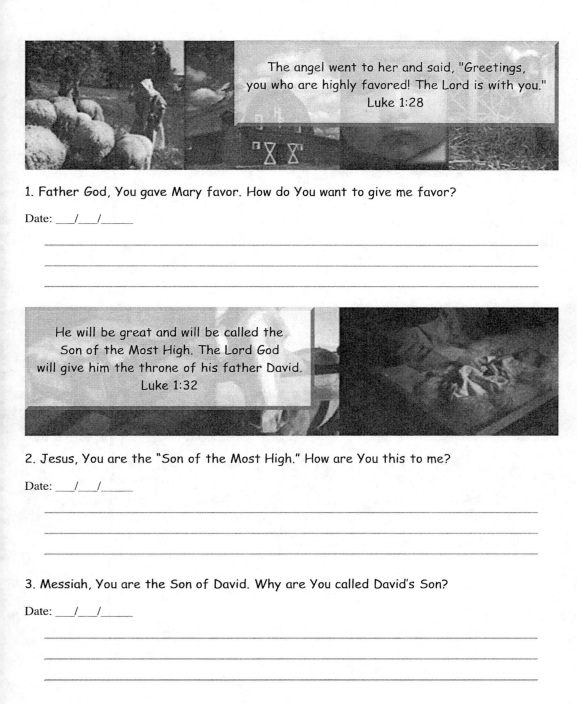

The angel went to her and said, "Greetings, you who are highly favored! The Lord is with you."
Luke 1:28

1. Father God, You gave Mary favor. How do You want to give me favor?

Date: ___/___/_____

_____
_____
_____

He will be great and will be called the Son of the Most High. The Lord God will give him the throne of his father David.
Luke 1:32

2. Jesus, You are the "Son of the Most High." How are You this to me?

Date: ___/___/_____

_____
_____
_____

3. Messiah, You are the Son of David. Why are You called David's Son?

Date: ___/___/_____

_____
_____
_____

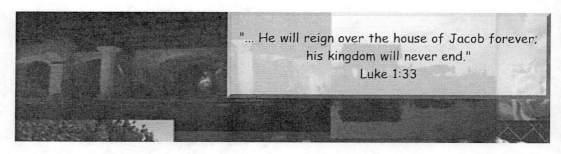

"... He will reign over the house of Jacob forever;
his kingdom will never end."
Luke 1:33

4. Christ, Your Kingdom will never end. How can I partner with You to bring Your Kingdom?

Date: ___/___/_____

_____
_____
_____
_____

"... For nothing is impossible with God."
Luke 1:37

5. Jesus, nothing is impossible for You. How can I trust You more?

Date: ___/___/_____

_____
_____
_____
_____

"I am the Lord's servant," Mary answered.
"May it be to me as you have said."
Then the angel left her.
Luke 1:38

6. Lord, Mary was Your servant. How am I Your servant?

Date: ___/___/_____

_____
_____
_____
_____

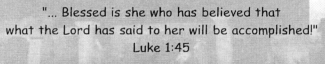

"... Blessed is she who has believed that
what the Lord has said to her will be accomplished!"
Luke 1:45

7. Abba Papa, I want to believe You will do what you say. What do You want me to believe?

Date: ___/___/_____

_____
_____
_____
_____

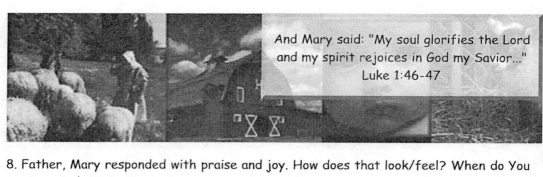

And Mary said: "My soul glorifies the Lord and my spirit rejoices in God my Savior..."
Luke 1:46-47

8. Father, Mary responded with praise and joy. How does that look/feel? When do You want me to have joy?

Date: ___/___/_____

_____

_____

_____

_____

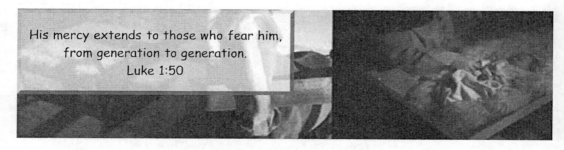

His mercy extends to those who fear him, from generation to generation.
Luke 1:50

9. Jesus, Your mercy keeps going generation to generation. How can I receive more of Your mercy?

Date: ___/___/_____

_____

_____

_____

_____

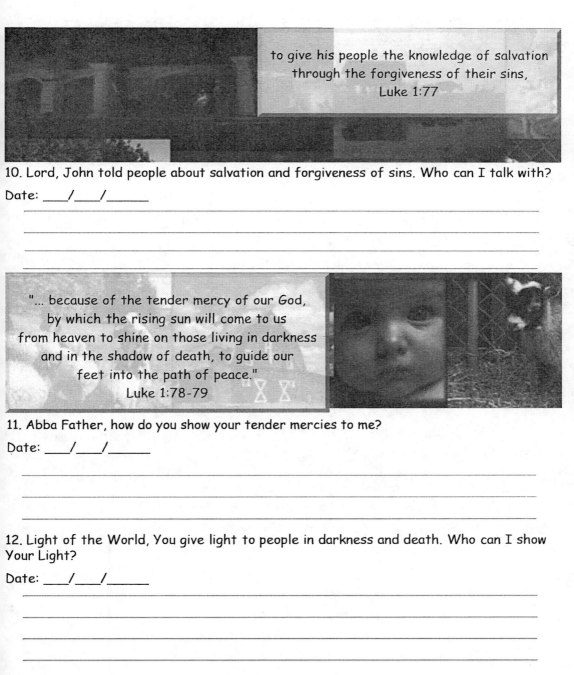

to give his people the knowledge of salvation
through the forgiveness of their sins,
Luke 1:77

10. Lord, John told people about salvation and forgiveness of sins. Who can I talk with?

Date: ___/___/_____

_____

_____

_____

_____

"... because of the tender mercy of our God,
by which the rising sun will come to us
from heaven to shine on those living in darkness
and in the shadow of death, to guide our
feet into the path of peace."
Luke 1:78-79

11. Abba Father, how do you show your tender mercies to me?

Date: ___/___/_____

_____

_____

_____

12. Light of the World, You give light to people in darkness and death. Who can I show Your Light?

Date: ___/___/_____

_____

_____

_____

_____

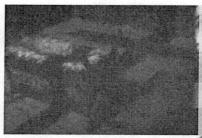

> But after he had considered this, an angel of
> the Lord appeared to him in a dream and said,
> "Joseph son of David, do not be afraid to take Mary
> home as your wife, because what is
> conceived in her is from the Holy Spirit."
> Matthew 1:20

13. Dad, You sent an angel to Joseph in a dream. How do You speak to me?

Date: ___/___/_____

_____
_____
_____
_____

> After Jesus was born in Bethlehem in Judea,
> during the time of King Herod, Magi from
> the east came to Jerusalem and asked,
> "Where is the one who has been born king of the Jews?
> We saw his star in the east and have come to worship him."
> Matthew 2:1-2

14. Messiah, the wise men came very far to worship you. How do you want me to worship You?

Date: ___/___/_____

_____
_____
_____
_____

On coming to the house, they saw the child with his mother Mary,
and they bowed down and worshiped him. Then they opened their
treasures and presented him with gifts of gold and of incense and of myrrh.
Matthew 2:11

15. Jesus, these wise and rich men knelt and worshiped You, a Baby! What can I give to You as worship?

Date: ___/___/_____

_____

_____

_____

_____

She gave birth to her firstborn, a son.
She wrapped him in cloths and placed him in a manger,
because there was no room for them in the inn.
Luke 2:7

16. Jesus, You were born a baby. How can I make room for You in me?

Date: ___/___/_____

_____

_____

_____

_____

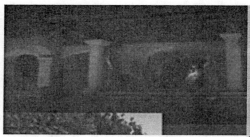

And there were shepherds living out in the fields nearby, keeping watch over their flocks at night. An angel of the Lord appeared to them, and the glory of the Lord shone around them, and they were terrified.
Luke 2:8-9

17. Father, You sent angels to poor shepherds. Why shepherds?

Date: ___/___/_____

Today in the town of David a Savior has been born to you; he is Christ the Lord.
Luke 2:11

18. Jesus, You are Savior, Messiah, and Lord. How are You my Savior? My Lord?

Date: ___/___/_____

"Glory to God in the highest, and on earth peace to men on whom his favor rests."
Luke 2:14

19. Jesus, all the angels sang, "Peace on earth". How can I bring Your peace?

Date: ___/___/_____

_____

_____

_____

_____

So they hurried off and found Mary and Joseph, and the baby, who was lying in the manger.
Luke 2:16

20. Lord, the shepherds ran. When do I run to You?

Date: ___/___/_____

_____

_____

_____

_____

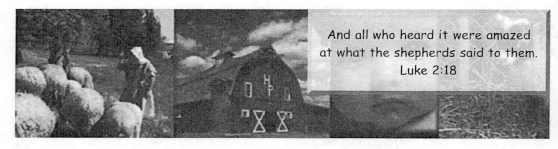

And all who heard it were amazed at what the shepherds said to them.
Luke 2:18

21. Father, everyone was so surprised and astonished. Why?

Date: ___/___/_____

_____
_____
_____
_____

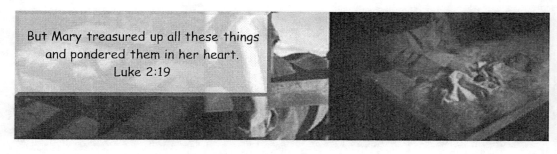

But Mary treasured up all these things and pondered them in her heart.
Luke 2:19

22. Jesus, Mary treasured things in her heart. How can I treasure things You say to me?

Date: ___/___/_____

_____
_____
_____
_____

When the parents brought in the child Jesus to do
for him what the custom of the Law required, Simeon
took him in his arms and praised God,
Luke 2:27-28

23. Jesus, You were only a baby! How do I wait for You, my Messiah?

Date: ___/___/_____

_____

_____

_____

_____

"... a light for revelation to the Gentiles
and for glory to your people Israel."
Luke 2:32

24. Light of the nations, how can I help people see Your light?

Date: ___/___/_____

_____

_____

_____

_____

Coming up to them at that very moment,
she gave thanks to God and spoke about
the child to all who were looking forward
to the redemption of Jerusalem.
Luke 2:38

25. Jesus, she talked to everyone about You. Who can I talk to about You?

Date: ___/___/_____

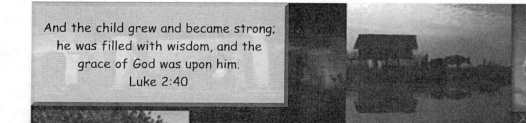

And the child grew and became strong;
he was filled with wisdom, and the
grace of God was upon him.
Luke 2:40

26. Dad, You gave Jesus wisdom and favor. What wisdom and favor do You want to give me?

Date: ___/___/_____

> "Then the King will say to those on his right, 'Come, you who are blessed by my Father; take your inheritance, the kingdom prepared for you since the creation of the world. For I was hungry and you gave me something to eat, I was thirsty and you gave me something to drink, I was a stranger and you invited me in...'"
> Matthew 25:34-35

27. Father, You bless us when we give food to hungry people. Who can I give to?

Date: ___/___/_____

_____

_____

_____

_____

28. Father, You give us Your kingdom when we give thirsty people a drink. Who can I give to?

Date: ___/___/_____

_____

_____

_____

_____

"'... When did we see you a stranger and invite you in, or needing clothes and clothe you? When did we see you sick or in prison and go to visit you?' "The King will reply, 'I tell you the truth, whatever you did for one of the least of these brothers of mine, you did for me.'"
Matthew 25:38-40

29. Jesus, You honor people who visit the sick. Who can I honor?

Date: ___/___/_____

30. Jesus, how do you want to use me to help those imprisoned?

Date: ___/___/_____

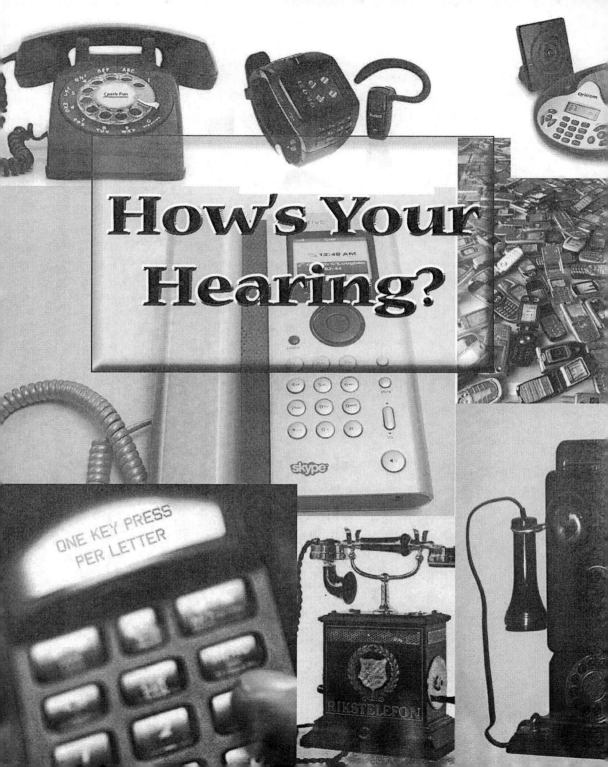

How's Your Hearing?

ONE KEY PRESS PER LETTER

RIKSTELEFON

Prayer is Listening and Talking

God loves to listen. He delights in our telling Him all the details of what happened in our day. He is never bored or too busy. He is always ready to listen to us. God also loves when we listen to Him.

Jesus is the Shepherd of the sheep. Did you know that a shepherd is the one who is responsible to make sure the sheep have enough food to eat? He also makes sure that the sheep are protected from any trouble or danger. Even if the shepherd has lots of sheep to watch, even 100, and just one sheep gets lost, the shepherd will go to find that one lost sheep. When He finds that sheep, He bandages him, and carries him in His arms.

Each shepherd has a certain sound to his voice. When a shepherd calls all His sheep to come and follow him, only his sheep obey. Other sheep, not in His sheepfold, don't follow Him. Why? Because they don't recognize the sound of His voice!

God loves to talk. He is called, "The Word of God." As we listen we learn to recognize his voice. We learn to obey Him because we are His sheep. Jesus is our Shepherd. He really feeds, protects and speaks to us.

This is the confidence we have in approaching God:
that if we ask anything according to his will, he hears us.
And if we know that he hears us--whatever
we ask--we know that we have what we asked of him.
1st John 5:14-15

1. Father, what is Your will for me?

Date: ___/___/_____

_____

_____

_____

_____

And I will do whatever you ask in my name,
so that the Son may bring glory to the Father.
John 14:13

2. Friend, You said I can ask You for anything in Your name. What do you want me to ask for now?

Date: ___/___/_____

_____

_____

_____

_____

You may ask me for anything in my name, and I will do it.
John 14:14

3. Jesus, I want to bring You glory and honor. So what could I ask for?

Date: ___/___/_____

_____

_____

_____

_____

In that day you will no longer ask me anything. I tell you the truth,
my Father will give you whatever you ask in my name.
John 16:23

4. Dear Father, I can pray directly to You. Why?

Date: ___/___/_____

_____

_____

_____

_____

The watchman opens the gate for him, and the sheep listen to his voice.
He calls his own sheep by name and leads them out.
John 10:3

5. Jesus, how do You lead me? What do You call me?

Date: ___/___/_____

_____
_____
_____
_____

When he has brought out all his own, he goes
on ahead of them, and his sheep follow him
because they know his voice.
John 10:4

6. Shepherd, what does Your voice sound like? How will I recognize it?

Date: ___/___/_____

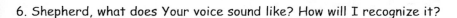
_____
_____
_____

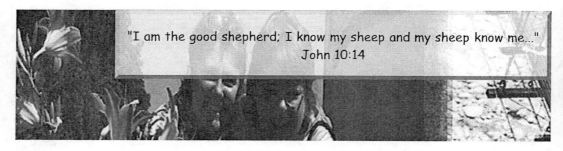

"I am the good shepherd; I know my sheep and my sheep know me..."
John 10:14

7. Jesus, how do You know me? How can I know You?

Date: ___/___/_____

_____

_____

_____

_____

But when you pray, go into your room,
close the door and pray to your Father,
who is unseen. Then your Father,
who sees what is done in secret, will reward you.
Matthew 6:6

8. Jesus, You want me to pray secretly. Why?

Date: ___/___/_____

_____

_____

_____

_____

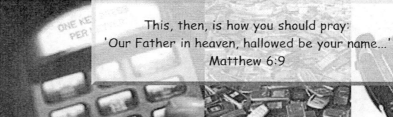

This, then, is how you should pray:
'Our Father in heaven, hallowed be your name...'
Matthew 6:9

9. Father, I want to honor Your name. How can I?

Date: ___/___/_____

_____

_____

_____

_____

Your kingdom come, your will be done on earth as it is in heaven.
Matthew 6:10

10. Daddy, how can I bring Your Kingdom on earth today?

Date: ___/___/_____

_____

_____

_____

_____

11. Father, today, what is Your will? How can I join Your prayers?

Date: ___/___/_____

_____

_____

_____

_____

Forgive us our debts, as we also have forgiven our debtors.
Matthew 6:12

12. Lord, sometimes people sin against me. Have I forgiven everyone?

Date: ___/___/_____

_____

_____

_____

_____

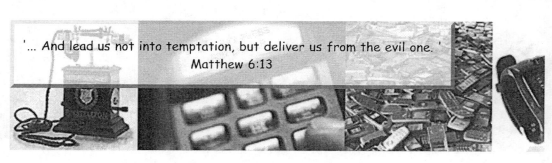

'... And lead us not into temptation, but deliver us from the evil one. '
Matthew 6:13

13. Jesus, sometimes I sin, but I don't want to. How can I stop sinning?

Date: ___/___/_____

_____

_____

_____

_____

But when you fast, put oil on your head and wash your face, so that it will not be obvious to men that you are fasting, but only to your Father, who is unseen; and your Father, who sees what is done in secret, will reward you.
Matthew 6:17-18

14. Dad, You want me to fast. Why? How can I?

Date: ___/___/_____

_____

_____

_____

_____

"Again, I tell you that if two of you on earth agree about anything you ask for, it will be done for you by my Father in heaven..."
Matthew 18:19

15. Abba, who can I pray with? What can we pray for?

Date: ___/___/_____

_____

_____

_____

_____

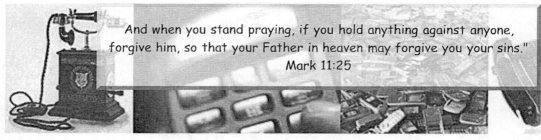

And when you stand praying, if you hold anything against anyone, forgive him, so that your Father in heaven may forgive you your sins."
Mark 11:25

16. Father, before I pray You want me to forgive people. Have I forgiven everyone?

Date: ___/___/_____

_____
_____
_____
_____

"If you believe, you will receive whatever you ask for in prayer."
Matthew 21:22

17. Daddy, before You answer my prayer You want me to believe You. How can I trust You more?

Date: ___/___/_____

_____
_____
_____
_____

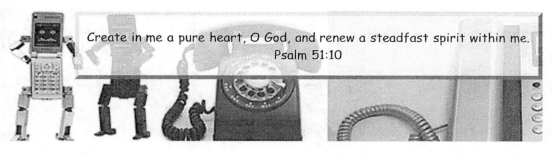

Create in me a pure heart, O God, and renew a steadfast spirit within me.
Psalm 51:10

18. Oh God, how do You want to make my heart clean and change how I think?

Date: ___/___/_____

_____
_____
_____
_____

Restore to me the joy of your salvation and grant me a willing spirit, to sustain me.
Psalm 51:12

19. Dad, how do You want me to obey You today?

Date: ___/___/_____

_____
_____
_____
_____

> "Therefore, if you are offering your gift at the altar and there remember that your brother has something against you, leave your gift there in front of the altar. First go and be reconciled to your brother; then come and offer your gift.
> Matthew 5:23-24

20. Papa, sometimes I sin towards people. Who do You want me to ask for forgiveness?

Date: ___/___/_____

_____

_____

_____

_____

> In the same way, the Spirit helps us in our weakness. We do not know what we ought to pray for, but the Spirit himself intercedes for us with groans that words cannot express.
> Romans 8:26

21. Holy Spirit, You want to help me pray. How? Why?

Date: ___/___/_____

_____

_____

_____

_____

22. Holy Spirit, You are praying for me right now. What are You praying?

Date: ___/___/_____

_____

_____

_____

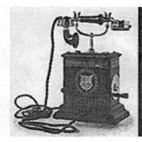
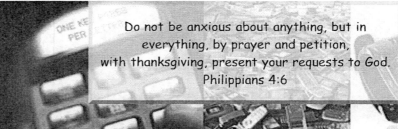

> Do not be anxious about anything, but in
> everything, by prayer and petition,
> with thanksgiving, present your requests to God.
> Philippians 4:6

23. Jesus, I want to thank You right now. Please show me all You did and do for me.

Date: ___/___/_____

> And my God will meet all your needs according to his glorious riches in Christ Jesus.
> Philippians 4:19

24. Abba Father, what do You want to give me?

Date: ___/___/_____

Cast all your anxiety on him because he cares for you.
1st Peter 5:7

25. Father, what worries can I give to You?

Date: ___/___/_____

_____
_____
_____
_____

We always thank God, the Father of our Lord Jesus Christ, when we pray for you,
Colossians 1:3

26. Papa, today who can I thank You for? How can I pray for them?

Date: ___/___/_____

_____
_____
_____
_____

If any of you lacks wisdom, he should ask God, who gives generously to all without finding fault, and it will be given to him.
James 1:5

27. God, I need Your wisdom. What do You want me to do with (person, decision, problem)?

Date: ___/___/_____

_____
_____
_____
_____

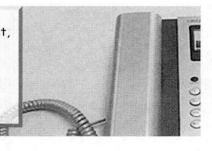

You want something but don't get it. You kill and covet, but you cannot have what you want.
You quarrel and fight. You do not have, because you do not ask God.
James 4:2

28. Dad, sometimes I forget to ask You. What can I ask for?

Date: ___/___/_____

_____
_____
_____
_____

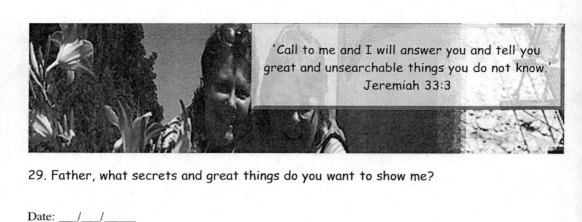

'Call to me and I will answer you and tell you
great and unsearchable things you do not know.'
Jeremiah 33:3

29. Father, what secrets and great things do you want to show me?

Date: ___/___/_____

_____

_____

_____

_____

... Or if he asks for a fish, will give him a snake?
If you, then, though you are evil, know how to give
good gifts to your children, how much more will your
Father in heaven give good gifts to those who ask him!
Matthew 7:10-11

30. Daddy, You always give me good gifts. What do You want to give me?

Date: ___/___/_____

_____

_____

_____

_____

Pure Laughter

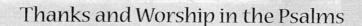

Thanks and Worship in the Psalms

Thankful hearts are happy hearts. What do you have that you haven't received? About your most prized possession—was it a gift from someone? Did you buy it with your own money? Where did you get the money? Where did they get the money? Did someone work for the money? All our abilities, talents, opportunities—everything is a gift from God our Father. Think about it. Everything—ultimately, every single thing we have comes from God.

We can be thankful for anything—for everything! The Bible says, "Give thanks in all things." No matter what we have, no matter what happens, God wants us to thank Him. He is so generous and kind to us. He cares about us. He watches all the big things AND all the little details of our lives.

Did you know that all of creation praises God? There is nothing, absolutely nothing, that He did not create. The sun and stars praise Him. Mountains, rivers, and fields praise Him. Trees and flowers praise him. Lions and elephants praise Him. Eagles and butterflies praise Him.

We thank and praise Him because He made us. As His children, we thank and praise Him even more. He not only made us, but He also saves us and lives inside us!

I will praise you, O Lord my God,
with all my heart;
I will glorify your name forever.
Psalm 86:12

1. Father, I want to worship You with my whole heart. How can I glorify Your name?

Date: ___/___/_____

2. Father, I give You glory and honor. How can I give You even more?

Date: ___/___/_____

All the nations you have made will come and worship before you, O Lord; they will bring glory to your name. For you are great and do marvelous deeds; you alone are God.
Psalm 86:9-10

3. Father, the nations will kneel before You. Why? How?

Date: ___/___/_____

_____

_____

_____

_____

4. Jesus, You are the only God. How are You my only God?

Date: ___/___/_____

_____

_____

_____

_____

The heavens praise your wonders, O Lord,
your faithfulness too,
in the assembly of the holy ones.
Psalm 89:5

5. You are faithful to me, Father. When have You been faithful to me?

Date: ___/___/_____

_____

_____

_____

It is good to praise the Lord and make music to your name, O Most High,
Psalm 92:1

6. Lord, it is good to praise You. What can I praise You for now?

Date: ___/___/_____

_____

_____

_____

7. God, You are the Most High God. You want us to sing praises to You. Why?

Date: ___/___/_____

_____

_____

_____

... to proclaim your love in the morning
and your faithfulness at night.
Psalm 92:2

8. Dad, at night You want me to talk about your faithfulness. Why?

Date: ___/___/_____

_____

_____

_____

Come, let us bow down in worship,
let us kneel before the Lord our Maker;
Psalm 95:6

9. Father, You want me to worship You. How can I worship You more?

Date: ___/___/_____

_____

_____

_____

10. Father, You want me to kneel and to bow down. Why?

Date: ___/___/_____

_____

_____

_____

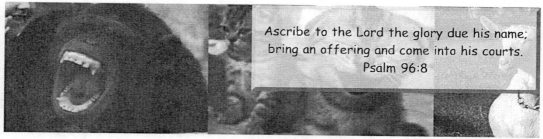

Ascribe to the Lord the glory due his name;
bring an offering and come into his courts.
Psalm 96:8

11. Daddy, You want me to bring an offering. What can I bring?

Date: ___/___/_____

_____

_____

_____

_____

12. Papa, how do angels give You glory? How can I give You glory?

Date: ___/___/_____

_____

_____

_____

_____

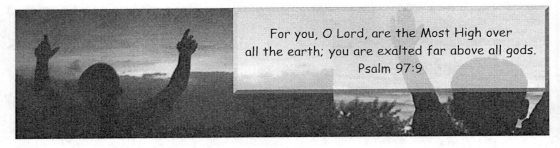

For you, O Lord, are the Most High over all the earth; you are exalted far above all gods.
Psalm 97:9

13. God, You are higher than all other gods. How much higher?

Date: ___/___/_____

_____

_____

_____

_____

Shout for joy to the Lord, all the earth, burst into jubilant song with music;
Psalm 98:4

14. Lord, You want me to shout for joy, why?

Date: ___/___/_____

_____

_____

_____

_____

Let the sea resound, and everything in it,
the world, and all who live in it.
Let the rivers clap their hands,
Psalm 98:7-8

15. Lord, the sea shouts Your praise. Why? What does it sound like?

Date: ___/___/_____

_____

_____

_____

_____

16. God, the rivers clap their hands in joy. Why? What does it sound like?

Date: ___/___/_____

_____

_____

_____

_____

17. Jesus, You want me to clap my hands in worship. Why?

Date: ___/___/_____

_____

_____

_____

_____

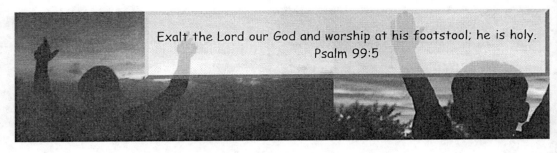

Exalt the Lord our God and worship at his footstool; he is holy.
Psalm 99:5

18. Lord, I want to lift You up. How does heaven exalt and lift You up?

Date: ___/___/_____

_____

_____

_____

_____

19. Lord, You want me to bow at Your feet. How are You Holy?

Date: ___/___/_____

_____

_____

_____

_____

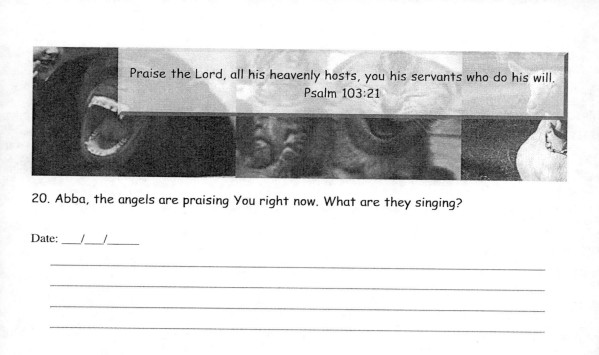

Praise the Lord, all his heavenly hosts, you his servants who do his will.
Psalm 103:21

20. Abba, the angels are praising You right now. What are they singing?

Date: ___/___/_____

_____

_____

_____

_____

Praise the Lord, all his works everywhere in his dominion. Praise the Lord, O my soul.
Psalm 103:22

21. Lord, the mountains and oceans praise You. How?

Date: ___/___/_____

_____

_____

_____

_____

Praise the Lord, O my soul. O Lord my God,
you are very great; you are clothed with
splendor and majesty. He wraps himself in
light as with a garment; he
stretches out the heavens like a tent
Psalm 104:1-2

22. Father, You are clothed with splendor, majesty and light. Would You show me this?

Date: ___/___/_____

_____

_____

_____

_____

23. Lord, how can I talk to my soul? What do You want me to say?

Date: ___/___/_____

_____

_____

_____

_____

Jesus declared, "Believe me, woman, a time is coming when you will worship the Father neither on this mountain nor in Jerusalem..."
John 4:21

24. Jesus, it does not matter where we worship You. Why not?

Date: ___/___/_____

_____

_____

_____

_____

... Yet a time is coming and has now come when the true worshipers will worship the Father in spirit and truth, for they are the kind of worshipers the Father seeks. God is spirit, and his worshipers must worship in spirit and in truth."
John 4:23-24

25. Daddy, You look for true worshipers, worshipers in spirit. How am I a true worshiper?

Date: ___/___/_____

_____

_____

_____

_____

26. Jesus, I want to worship in spirit and in truth. What truth do you want to show me?

Date: ___/___/_____

_____

_____

_____

_____

Jesus replied: "'Love the Lord your God with all your heart and with all your soul and with all your mind...'"
Matthew 22:37

27. Jesus, You want me to love You with my whole being. Why?

Date: ___/___/_____

_____

_____

_____

_____

28. Jesus, You want me to love You with my whole heart. How can I?

Date: ___/___/_____

_____

_____

_____

_____

He answered: "Love the Lord your God with all your heart and with all your soul and with all your strength and with all your mind; and, 'Love your neighbor as yourself."
Luke 10:27

29. Dad, You want me to love You with my whole mind. How can I?

Date: ___/___/_____

_____

_____

_____

_____

Jesus replied: " 'Love the Lord your God with all your heart and with all your soul and with all your mind.' This is the first and greatest commandment..."
Matthew 22:37-38

30. Jesus, loving You is Your greatest command. Why is that the greatest?

Date: ___/___/_____

_____

_____

_____

_____

Holy Spirit Fruit

Sweet and Ripe

Imagine your favorite fruit. It's perfectly ripe and sweet. Mmmm, yummy! Remember when you took a bite of a fruit that looked good, but was rotten or bitter? Ulllll, yuk!

Jesus left the earth and went to heaven. Then He sent His Spirit to come to be inside us. His Spirit helps us from the inside out. We let the Holy Spirit direct our lives by letting Jesus be our King. The Holy Spirit connects with our spirit. Our spirit controls our self - our mind, our emotions, our will, our bodies. This is how we experience the fruit of the Spirit.

Apple trees produce apples. Orange trees produce oranges. Banana trees produce bananas. In the same way the Holy Spirit, through our spirit, produces His fruit inside us. Others can see this fruit in our lives.

Who are the happiest people in the world? I think the happiest people in the world are not those weathly with lots of toys or clothes. The happiest people in the world are ones who experience the fruit of the Spirit inside. They have joy and peace deep inside. They know how good it feels to show love and compassion to people. They feel so good when they are patient and gentle. They do not feel good when they are irritated, anxious, selfish or have self-pity. They are faithful to make good choices. They do what is right, kind and good. Their spirit controls their self and the Holy Spirit directs their spirit.

But the fruit of the Spirit is love, joy, peace, patience, kindness, goodness, faithfulness...
Galatians 5:22

1. Holy Spirit, why are these all fruit? love, joy, peace, patience, kindness...

Date: ___/___/_____

2. Father, You want me to have fruit. Why?

Date: ___/___/_____

But the fruit of the Spirit is love, joy, peace, patience, kindness, goodness, faithfulness...
Galatians 5:22

3. Abba Daddy, You want to help me love better. Who?

Date: ___/___/_____

_____

_____

_____

_____

4. Papa, You want me to be joyful. Why?

Date: ___/___/_____

_____

_____

_____

_____

5. Holy Spirit, You want to help me be more patient. When am I not patient?

Date: ___/___/_____

_____

_____

_____

_____

6. Dad, You want me to be kind. Who? How?

Date: ___/___/_____

_____
_____
_____
_____

7. Father, You want to help me to be like You. How can I be good?

Date: ___/___/_____

_____
_____
_____
_____

8. Daddy, You want me to be faithful. When am I faithful?

Date: ___/___/_____

_____
_____
_____
_____

... gentleness and self-control.
Against such things there is no law.
Galatians 5:23

9. Jesus, You help me to be gentle. How can I be gentle like You?

Date: ___/___/_____

_____

_____

_____

10. Holy Spirit, I want to be self-controlled. How does Your Spirit help my spirit to control my body and soul?

Date: ___/___/_____

_____

_____

_____

_____

11. Holy Spirit, You want to help me have this fruit. How do You help me have fruit?

Date: ___/___/_____

_____

_____

_____

_____

When he saw the crowds, he had compassion
on them, because they were harassed
and helpless, like sheep without a shepherd.
Matthew 9:36

12. Messiah, to see like You see is very important. Who do you want to show me?

Date: ___/___/_____

_____

_____

_____

_____

13. Jesus, You want to help me feel compassion. Who do you feel compassion for?

Date: ___/___/_____

_____

_____

_____

_____

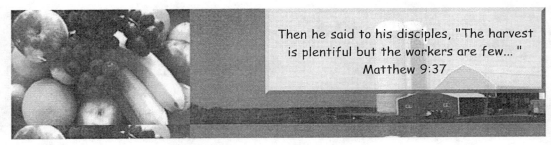

Then he said to his disciples, "The harvest is plentiful but the workers are few... "
Matthew 9:37

14. Jesus, My friends do not know You. How can I help them?

Date: ___/___/_____

15. Father, You want people to labor with You. How can I?

Date: ___/___/_____

16. Abba, You want me to pray for more laborers. Who can I pray for?

Date: ___/___/_____

Therefore, as God's chosen people, holy
and dearly loved, clothe yourselves with
compassion, kindness, humility,
gentleness and patience.
Colossians 3:12

17. God, why did You choose me?

Date: ___/___/_____

18. Papa, how can I put on tender mercies?

Date: ___/___/_____

19. Jesus, why am I holy and dearly loved?

Date: ___/___/_____

_____

_____

_____

_____

20. Dad, how can I be kind today?

Date: ___/___/_____

_____

_____

_____

_____

21. Jesus, how can I be humble like You?

Date: ___/___/_____

_____

_____

_____

_____

Therefore, as God's chosen people, holy and dearly loved, clothe yourselves with compassion, kindness, humility, gentleness and patience.
Colossians 3:12

22. Holy Spirit, how do You help me to be gentle?

Date: ___/___/_____

23. Father, You want me to be patient. When?

Date: ___/___/_____

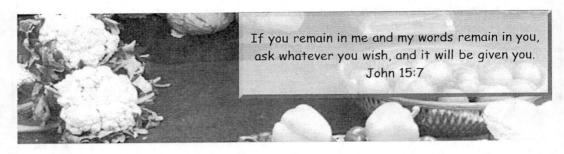

If you remain in me and my words remain in you,
ask whatever you wish, and it will be given you.
John 15:7

24. Jesus, how can I remain in You?

Date: ___/___/_____

_____

_____

_____

_____

25. Jesus, how do Your words abide in me?

Date: ___/___/_____

_____

_____

_____

_____

This is to my Father's glory, that you bear much fruit, showing yourselves to be my disciples.
John 15:8

26. Jesus, am I Your true disciple? Why?

Date: ___/___/_____

_____

_____

_____

_____

"As the Father has loved me, so have I loved you.
Now remain in my love. If you obey my commands,
you will remain in my love, just as I have
obeyed my Father's commands and remain in his love..."
John 15:9-10

27. Jesus, I want to obey You. I want to receive more of Your love. How can I?

Date: ___/___/_____

_____

_____

_____

_____

My command is this: Love each
other as I have loved you.
John 15:12

28. Dear Jesus, I want to love people like You love me. How can I?

Date: ___/___/_____

_____

_____

_____

_____

Greater love has no one than this,
that he lay down his life for his friends.
John 15:13

29. Lord Jesus, how can I give my life to people? Who can I give my life to?

Date: ___/___/_____

_____

_____

_____

_____

You are my friends if you do what I command.
John 15:14

30. Jesus, how am I Your friend?

Date: ___/___/_____

Born To Die Born to Rise

The Easter Story

Jesus was born at Christmas to die & rise again. His death and resurrection are celebrated at Easter. Jesus was slapped. He was whipped with ropes that had sharp pieces that ripped His skin. The Bible says that this paid for our healing. He was spit on. His clothes were stripped off. He was laughed at. At night he was tired and cold. Later he was hungry, thirsty, and exhausted. People made him carry a huge heavy cross. They pounded nails into his wrists and feet.

When Jesus died, He said, "It is finished." All that is needed for salvation–to be born again, to be set free, to be healed, for body and soul to prosper. All of salvation was purchased on the cross, paid in full!

Strong soldiers guarded Jesus' tomb. A monstrous stone was rolled uphill blocking the entrance to the tomb. A cloth, as long as a soccer field, was wrapped around Jesus. About 100 pounds of spices were soaked into the cloth. All of Jesus followers ran away when He was killed.

Three days after Jesus died He came back to life. Jesus was gone. His tomb was empty. It is still empty! Angels stayed to tell everyone that Jesus had risen from the dead. Jesus wanted everyone to know that He really had risen, so He let many people see Him. Once, more than 500 people saw Jesus at the same time.

Historical tradition says of Jesus 12 followers were killed because they declared Jesus rose from the dead. Their deaths prove they believed Jesus really is the Living God. At Easter, we celebrate that Jesus came back to life. Jesus is alive right now. That's why we can have a relationship with Him. He's alive!

They spit on him, and took the staff and struck him on the head again and again.
Matthew 27:30

1. Jesus, You are God. Why did You let people spit on You? How can I honor You?

Date: ___/___/_____

After that, he appeared to more than five hundred of the brothers at the same time, most of whom are still living, though some have fallen asleep.
1st Corinthians 15:6

2. Wow Lord, 500 people saw You! Why did You let so many people see You?

Date: ___/___/_____

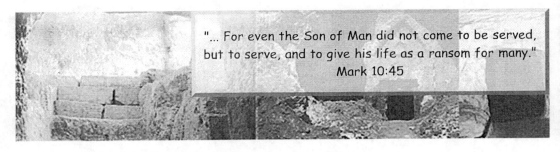

"... For even the Son of Man did not come to be served, but to serve, and to give his life as a ransom for many."
Mark 10:45

3. Lord Jesus Christ, You came to serve. Who can I serve?

Date: ___/___/_____

_____

_____

_____

_____

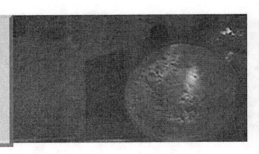

The Lord turned and looked straight at Peter. Then Peter remembered the word the Lord had spoken to him: "Before the rooster crows today, you will disown me three times." And he went outside and wept bitterly.
Luke 22:61-62

4. Jesus, You looked at Peter. What do you feel when I mess up?

Date: ___/___/_____

_____

_____

_____

_____

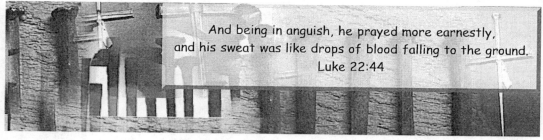

And being in anguish, he prayed more earnestly,
and his sweat was like drops of blood falling to the ground.
Luke 22:44

5. Jesus, You sweat drops of blood. Why did you love me this much?

Date: ___/___/_____

_____

_____

_____

_____

Now the betrayer had arranged a signal with them:
"The one I kiss is the man; arrest him."
Going at once to Jesus, Judas said,
"Greetings, Rabbi!" and kissed him.
Matthew 26:48-49

6. Jesus, Judas betrayed You by kissing You. How can I never betray You?

Date: ___/___/_____

_____

_____

_____

_____

"... Do you think I cannot call on my Father, and he will at once put at my disposal more than twelve legions of angels? But how then would the Scriptures be fulfilled that say it must happen in this way?"
Matthew 26:53-54

7. Jesus, Your Father would give 1000's of angels to protect You. Why didn't You ask Him?

Date: ___/___/_____

_____
_____
_____
_____

Dogs have surrounded me; a band of evil men has encircled me, they have pierced my hands and my feet. I can count all my bones; people stare and gloat over me. They divide my garments among them and cast lots for my clothing.
Psalm 22:16-18

8. Jesus, You let people take Your clothes. Why did You take my shame?

Date: ___/___/_____

_____
_____
_____
_____

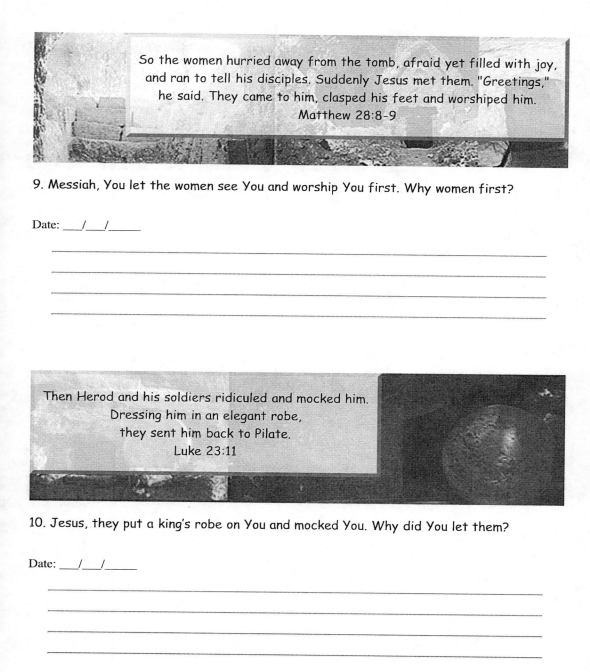

So the women hurried away from the tomb, afraid yet filled with joy, and ran to tell his disciples. Suddenly Jesus met them. "Greetings," he said. They came to him, clasped his feet and worshiped him.
Matthew 28:8-9

9. Messiah, You let the women see You and worship You first. Why women first?

Date: ___/___/_____

_____

_____

_____

_____

Then Herod and his soldiers ridiculed and mocked him.
Dressing him in an elegant robe,
they sent him back to Pilate.
Luke 23:11

10. Jesus, they put a king's robe on You and mocked You. Why did You let them?

Date: ___/___/_____

_____

_____

_____

_____

When he had received the drink, Jesus said, "It is finished." With that, he bowed his head and gave up his spirit.
John 19:30

11. Christ, You said, "It is finished." How does this affect me?

Date: ___/___/_____

_____

_____

_____

_____

"... and then twisted together a crown of thorns and set it on his head. They put a staff in his right hand and knelt in front of him and mocked him. "Hail, king of the Jews!" they said.
Matthew 27:29

12. Jesus, why a crown of thorns?

Date: ___/___/_____

_____

_____

_____

_____

So Pilate decided to grant their demand.
He released the man who had been thrown
into prison for insurrection and murder,
the one they asked for,
and surrendered Jesus to their will.
Luke 23:24-25

13. Daddy, why do You let evil things happen? Why didn't You rescue Jesus?

Date: ___/___/_____

_____
_____
_____
_____

I am poured out like water, and all my bones
are out of joint. My heart has turned
to wax; it has melted away within me.
Psalm 22:14

14. Jesus, when You hung on the cross, what did You feel for me then?

Date: ___/___/_____

_____
_____
_____
_____

While they were wondering about this, suddenly two men in clothes that gleamed like lightning stood beside them.
Luke 24:4

15. Jesus, where are Your angels now? How are they helping me?

Date: ___ / ___ / _____

_____
_____
_____
_____

"Father, if you are willing, take this cup from me; yet not my will, but yours be done." An angel from heaven appeared to him and strengthened him.
Luke 22:42-43

16. Father, You didn't stop people from killing Jesus. Why did You love me this much?

Date: ___ / ___ / _____

_____
_____
_____
_____

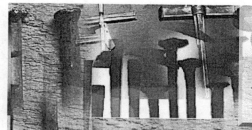

It was now about the sixth hour, and
darkness came over the whole land until
the ninth hour, for the sun stopped shining.
And the curtain of the temple was torn in two.
Luke 23:44-45

17. It suddenly turned pitch dark during lunch! Papa, Why did You do that?

Date: ___/___/_____

_____

_____

_____

_____

And at the ninth hour Jesus cried
out in a loud voice, "Eloi, Eloi, lama sabachthani?"
--which means, "My God, my God, why have you forsaken me?"
Mark 15:34

18. Daddy, You left Jesus. Will You ever leave me?

Date: ___/___/_____

_____

_____

_____

_____

At that moment the curtain of the temple
was torn in two from top to bottom.
The earth shook and the rocks split.
Matthew 27:51

19. Jesus, when You died the curtain in the temple was torn. How does this impact me?

Date: ___/___/_____

_____

_____

_____

_____

When the centurion and those with him
who were guarding Jesus saw the earthquake
and all that had happened, they were
terrified, and exclaimed, "Surely he was the Son of God!"
Matthew 27:54

20. Dad, You made the earth quake when Jesus died. Why?

Date: ___/___/_____

_____

_____

_____

_____

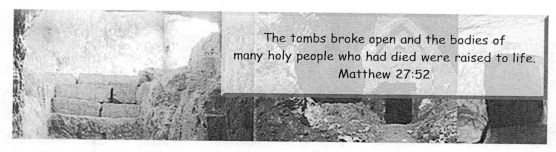

The tombs broke open and the bodies of many holy people who had died were raised to life.
Matthew 27:52

21. Jesus, after You died, other dead people walked around. Why? Who?

Date: ___/___/_____

_____

_____

_____

_____

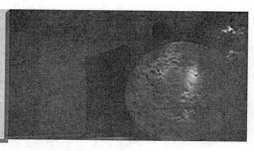

There was a violent earthquake, for an angel of the Lord came down from heaven and, going to the tomb, rolled back the stone and sat on it. His appearance was like lightning, and his clothes were white as snow.
Matthew 28:2-3

22. Papa God, You sent an angel to roll the huge stone away. Why?

Date: ___/___/_____

_____

_____

_____

_____

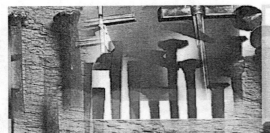

But he was pierced for our transgressions, he was crushed for our iniquities; the punishment that brought us peace was upon him, and by his wounds we are healed.
Isaiah 53:5

23. Jehovah-Rahpe, Healer, how do You want to heal me and others? Who do You want me to heal?

Date: ___/___/_____

_____

_____

_____

_____

Then their eyes were opened and they recognized him, and he disappeared from their sight.
Luke 24:31

24. Messiah, You suddenly let them recognize You. How do you want to reveal Yourself to me?

Date: ___/___/_____

_____

_____

_____

_____

Look at my hands and my feet. It is
I myself! Touch me and see; a ghost
does not have flesh and bones,
as you see I have."
Luke 24:39

25. Jesus, why did You eat? How can I touch You?

Date: ___/___/_____

_____
_____
_____
_____

But Christ has indeed been raised from the dead,
the firstfruits of those who have fallen asleep.
1st Corinthians 15:20

26. Jesus, will I be raised to life with You? Why?

Date: ___/___/_____

_____
_____
_____
_____

For we know that our old self was crucified with him so that the body of sin might be done away with, that we should no longer be slaves to sin--
Romans 6:6

27. Jesus, I don't want to be a slave to any sin. How do you want to help me?

Date: ___/___/_____

_____

_____

_____

_____

Don't you know that when you offer yourselves to someone to obey him as slaves, you are slaves to the one whom you obey--whether you are slaves to sin, which leads to death, or to obedience, which leads to righteousness?
Romans 6:16

28. Jesus, how does my sin lead to death? How can I choose life?

Date: ___/___/_____

_____

_____

_____

_____

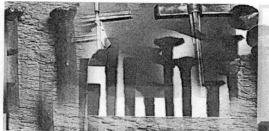

He did not enter by means of the blood of goats and calves; but he entered the Most Holy Place once for all by his own blood, having obtained eternal redemption.
Hebrews 9:12

29. Jesus, why did You have to die? Wasn't there an easier way to pay for my sin?

Date: ___/___/_____

_____

_____

_____

_____

In fact, the law requires that nearly everything be cleansed with blood, and without the shedding of blood there is no forgiveness.
Hebrews 9:22

30. Christ, You need blood to forgive sin. Why?

Date: ___/___/_____

_____

_____

_____

_____

Upside Down Radical!

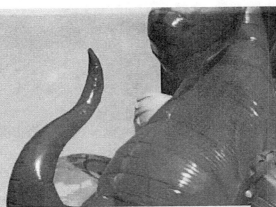

The Very First Church

Have you ever wondered, "When was the first church? What was it like?" I guess God must have thought people like us might wonder about that. So He wrote about it in the Bible. In the New Testament, the book of Acts, amazing things happened! It begins by summarizing what Jesus taught about from His resurrection to His ascension. He taught about the kingdom.

Then the Holy Spirit came with fire and roaring wind. People from many languages heard the good news all in their own language. Peter taught for the first time and thousands of people became believers in Jesus. It tells what happened to the first Christians. It helps us learn what was important to them.

Paul got radically converted and then took 3 missionary journeys. We see who the Holy Spirit is and how He established the Church. We see how we are to live!

Suddenly, there was a sound from heaven like the roaring of a mighty windstorm in the skies above them, and it filled the house where they were meeting.
Acts 2:2

1. Holy Spirit, You came suddenly, not slowly. How do you want to come to me now?

Date: ___/___/_____

_____
_____
_____
_____

Then, what looked like flames or tongues of fire appeared and settled on each of them.
Acts 2:3

2. Spirit of God, You put flames of fire on people's heads. How can I be more on fire?

Date: ___/___/_____

_____
_____
_____
_____

Then, what looked like flames or tongues
of fire appeared and settled on each of them.
Acts 2:3

3. Teacher, how do You put flames on us now?

Date: ___/___/_____

_____

_____

_____

_____

4. Holy Spirit, would You fill me right now?

Date: ___/___/_____

_____

_____

_____

_____

When they heard this sound, they came running to see what it was all about, and they were bewildered to hear their own languages being spoken by the believers.
Acts 2:6

5. Father God, people were speaking and hearing lots of languages. What languages do You want to give me?

Date: ___/___/_____

_____
_____
_____
_____

But others in the crowd were mocking. "They're drunk, that's all!" they said.
Acts 2:13

6. Holy Spirit, some people thought the apostles were drunk. Why? How can I drink You?

Date: ___/___/_____

_____
_____
_____
_____

"In the last days, God said, I will pour out my Spirit upon all people. Your sons and daughters will prophesy, your young men will see visions, and your old men will dream dreams..."
Acts 2:17

7. Comforter, You want me to prophesy also. To who? What should I say?

Date: ___/___/_____

_____

_____

_____

_____

8. Spirit of God, You want to show me visions. Why? What do You want to show me now?

Date: ___/___/_____

_____

_____

_____

_____

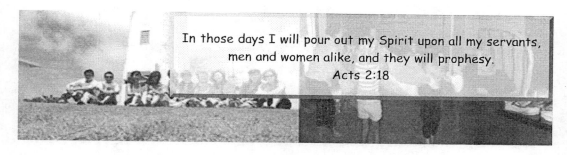

In those days I will pour out my Spirit upon all my servants,
men and women alike, and they will prophesy.
Acts 2:18

9. Lord, You want me to be your servant. Why? How can I serve You today?

Date: ___/___/_____

10. Abba Daddy, how can I serve my family today?

Date: ___/___/_____

11. Holy Spirit, who can I prophesy to? What?

Date: ___/___/_____

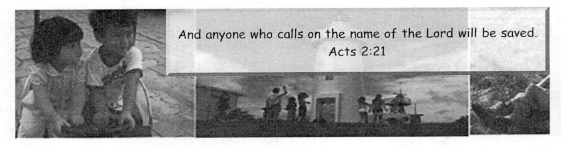

And anyone who calls on the name of the Lord will be saved.
Acts 2:21

12. Jesus, You want people to know You. You want people to have eternal life. Who do You want me to talk with?

Date: ___/___/_____

_____
_____
_____
_____

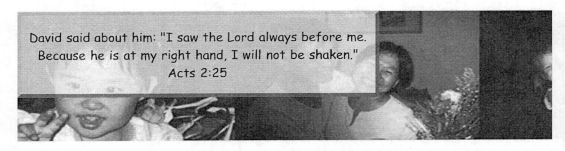

David said about him: "I saw the Lord always before me. Because he is at my right hand, I will not be shaken."
Acts 2:25

13. Jesus, I want to always see You. What do You want to show me now?

Date: ___/___/_____

_____
_____
_____
_____

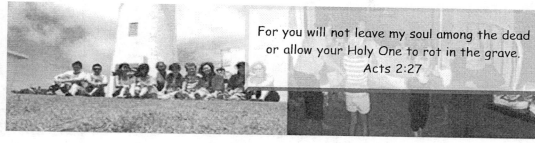

For you will not leave my soul among the dead
or allow your Holy One to rot in the grave.
Acts 2:27

14. Daddy, You raised Jesus from the dead. Why? You will raise me from the dead. Why?

Date: ___/___/_____

_____

_____

_____

David was looking into the future and predicting the Messiah's resurrection. He was saying that the Messiah would not be left among the dead and that his body would not rot in the grave.
Acts 2:31

15. Father God, You told of the Resurrection 1,000 years before Jesus was born. Why?

Date: ___/___/_____

_____

_____

_____

16. Jesus, You are the Messiah. Why? What does that mean to me?

Date: ___/___/_____

_____

_____

_____

Peter's words convicted them deeply,
and they said to him and to the other apostles,
"Brothers, what should we do?"
Acts 2:37

17. Papa, I want my words to touch people deeply. How can I?

Date: ___/___/_____

_____

_____

_____

_____

Peter replied, "Each of you must turn from your sins
and turn to God, and be baptized in the name of
Jesus Christ for the forgiveness of your sins.
Then you will receive the gift of the Holy Spirit..."
Acts 2:38

18. Jesus, You want Christians to be baptized. Why is baptism important to You?

Date: ___/___/_____

_____

_____

_____

_____

19. Holy Spirit, how can I receive You?

Date: ___/___/_____

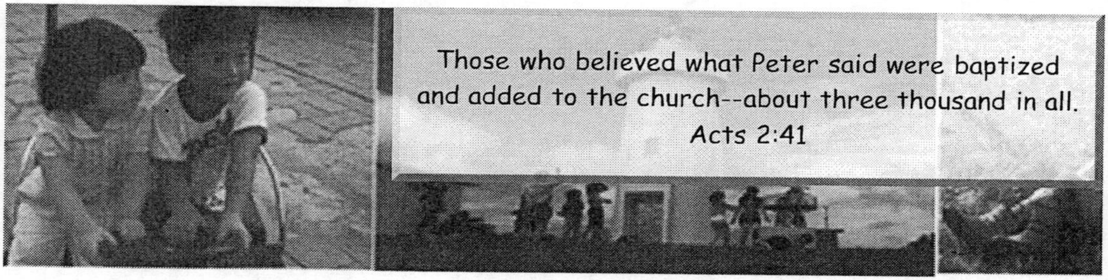

_____

_____

_____

_____

Those who believed what Peter said were baptized
and added to the church--about three thousand in all.
Acts 2:41

20. Lord, people sometimes worshiped with other believers. Why not worship only by myself?

Date: ___/___/_____

_____

_____

_____

_____

> They joined with the other believers and
> devoted themselves to the apostles' teaching
> and fellowship, sharing in the
> Lord's Supper and in prayer.
> Acts 2:42

21. Lord, You want me to devote myself to the Bible. How can I? Why?

Date: ___/___/_____

_____

_____

_____

_____

22. Jesus, You want me to share in the breaking of bread. With who?

Date: ___/___/_____

_____

_____

_____

_____

23. Father, You love to talk with me. How can I devote myself to prayer?

Date: ___/___/_____

_____

_____

_____

_____

A deep sense of awe came over them all,
and the apostles performed many
miraculous signs and wonders.
Acts 2:43

24. Daddy, You want to use me to do miracles. Wow! What miracles today? Why me?

Date: ___/___/_____

25. Lord, how can I see more miracles now?

Date: ___/___/_____

They sold their possessions and shared
the proceeds with those in need.
Acts 2:45

26. Jesus, You want me to be generous. Who can I give to? What can I give?

Date: ___/___/_____

_____

_____

_____

_____

They worshiped together at the Temple each day,
met in homes for the Lord's Supper,
and shared their meals with great joy and generosity...
Acts 2:46

27. Holy Spirit, how can I live in unity and community?

Date: ___/___/_____

_____

_____

_____

_____

28. Jesus, how can I eat with joy?

Date: ___/___/_____

_____
_____
_____
_____

... all the while praising God and enjoying the goodwill of all the people.
And each day the Lord added to their group those who were being saved.
Acts 2:47

29. Father, how do You want to give me favor will all the people?

Date: ___/___/_____

_____
_____
_____
_____

... all the while praising God and enjoying the goodwill of all the people. And each day the Lord added to their group those who were being saved.
Acts 2:47

30. Christ, I want to see people saved everyday like they did. How can I?

Date: ___/___/_____

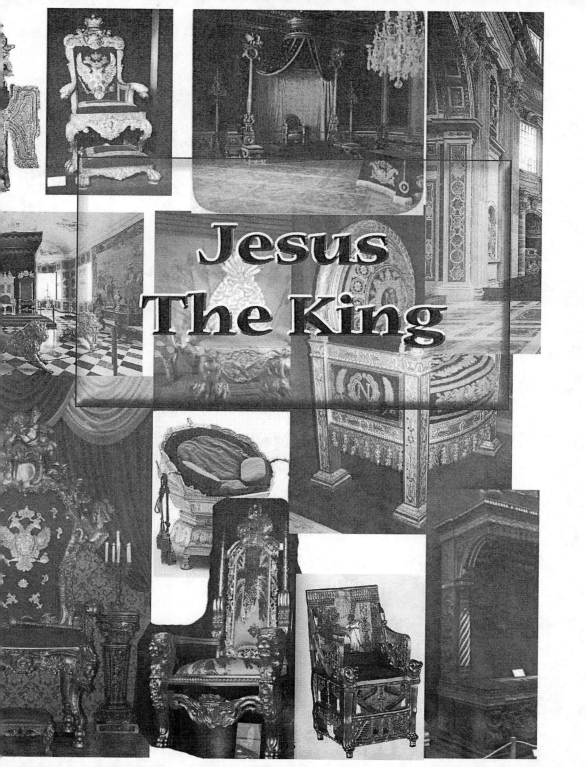

Jesus
The King

The King and His Kingdom

God our Father had all the authority. He gave all the authority to Jesus. In both heaven and on earth Jesus has all authority. Jesus is King over everything, everywhere.

Jesus can speak words and create worlds. Jesus' words created everything. Jesus words healed people. Jesus gives us His same authority. Jesus told us to use His name. We stand in Jesus' authority when we use Jesus name to declare. The Kingdom of God is God's right to be Ruler of everything. Jesus Christ is the King. Not everyone says Jesus is their King. But Jesus is still King.

Every time we hear truth about God, we make choices. We can choose to receive the truth. We can choose to obey and live it. When we choose good things, we show we are good soil. Sometimes it is hard to choose. But Jesus and His Kingdom are worth it. No matter what we give up, Christ and His Kingdom are worth it. Wow! What a valuable treasure! To show by our choices that Jesus Christ is our King, the King over all other kings and rulers!

Jesus' Kingdom is already established in heaven. In heaven everyone knows that Jesus Christ is the King. He reigns Supreme. He wants every person to honor Him. He wants us to obey Him completely. When we believe He is King and that He died for our sins we are born spiritually. We are seated in heaven with Him. He gives us an incredible privilege - to work with Him to establish His Kingdom on earth. He gives us all the authority and all the keys we need!

We bring the Kingdom of God wherever we go when Jesus is our Lord and Savior and we follow Him as His disciples. Bringing Jesus' Kingdom sometimes happens slowly like a mustard seed, the tiniest of seeds, but grows into one of the biggest trees. Sometimes His Kingdom comes suddenly!

Then Jesus came to them and said,
"All authority in heaven and on
earth has been given to me..."
Matthew 28:18

1. Jesus, You have all authority. You give me authority. Why? How can I be a good steward?

Date: ___/___/_____

_____

_____

_____

Therefore go and make disciples of all nations,
baptizing them in the name of the Father
and of the Son and of the Holy Spirit.
Matthew 28:19

2. Lord Jesus, You tell me to go and make disciples. What nations do You want me to disciple?

Date: ___/___/_____

_____

_____

_____

3. Teacher, who do You want me to disciple right now? What should I do?

Date: ___/___/_____

_____

_____

_____

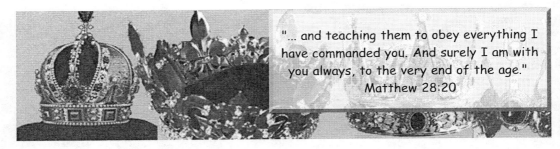

"... and teaching them to obey everything I
have commanded you. And surely I am with
you always, to the very end of the age."
Matthew 28:20

4. Dear Jesus, You are with me always. Why?

Date: ___/___/_____

_____

_____

_____

_____

Which is easier: to say to the paralytic, 'Your sins are forgiven,'
or to say, 'Get up, take your mat and walk'? But that you may know that
the Son of Man has authority on earth to forgive sins..."
He said to the paralytic, "I tell you, get up, take your mat and go home."
Mark 2:9-11

5. Jesus, You forgive our sins and heal us. Why do You both forgive and heal?

Date: ___/___/_____

_____

_____

_____

_____

> Which is easier: to say to the paralytic, 'Your sins are forgiven,' or to say, 'Get up, take your mat and walk'? But that you may know that the Son of Man has authority on earth to forgive sins..." He said to the paralytic, "I tell you, get up, take your mat and go home." Mark 2:9-11

6. Christ, You healed the man so everyone would know that You forgive sins. Why?

Date: ___/___/_____

_____

_____

_____

_____

7. Jesus, You want to heal people today so everyone will know You still forgive sins. Who do You want me to heal?

Date: ___/___/_____

_____

_____

_____

_____

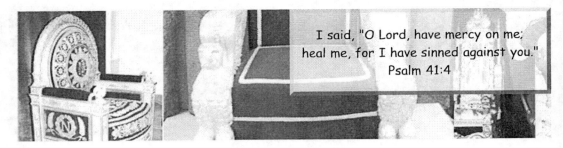

I said, "O Lord, have mercy on me; heal me, for I have sinned against you."
Psalm 41:4

8. Lord, in Your mercy You want to heal me. Heal who? Heal what?

Date: ___/___/_____

_____

_____

_____

_____

... who forgives all your sins and heals all your diseases,
Psalm 103:3

9. God, You forgive all my sins and heal all my diseases. How can I help others receive forgiveness and healing?

Date: ___/___/_____

_____

_____

_____

_____

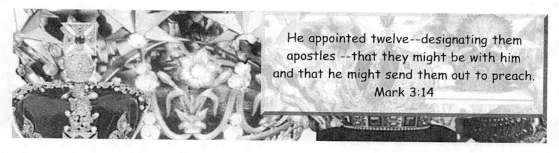

He appointed twelve--designating them apostles --that they might be with him and that he might send them out to preach.
Mark 3:14

10. Jesus, You want me to spend time with you. How can I? When? Where?

Date: ___/___/_____

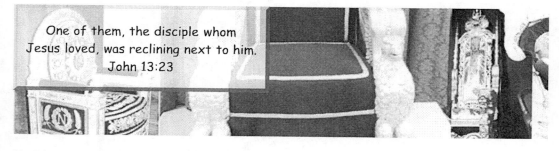

One of them, the disciple whom Jesus loved, was reclining next to him.
John 13:23

11. Jesus, I want to lean on You like John did. How can I?

Date: ___/___/_____

When Jesus had called the Twelve together, he gave them power and authority to drive out all demons and to cure diseases, and he sent them out to preach the kingdom of God and to heal the sick.
Luke 9:1-2

12. Messiah, You give me great power and authority. What do you want me to do?

Date: ___/___/_____

_____

_____

_____

_____

13. Jesus, I want my friends to know You. How can I show them Your kingdom?

Date: ___/___/_____

_____

_____

_____

_____

14. Jehovah-Raphe, Healer, You love to heal sick people. Who can I heal?

Date: ___/___/_____

_____

_____

_____

_____

I tell you the truth, anyone who has faith in me will do what I have been doing. He will do even greater things than these, because I am going to the Father. And I will do whatever you ask in my name, so that the Son may bring glory to the Father. You may ask me for anything in my name, and I will do it.
John 14:12-14

15. Jesus, You told me to do greater things than You did. What things? Why?

Date: ___/___/_____

_____

_____

_____

_____

16. Jesus, what greater things do You want me to ask You for?

Date: ___/___/_____

_____

_____

_____

_____

He told them another parable: "The kingdom of heaven is like a mustard seed, which a man took and planted in his field. Though it is the smallest of all your seeds, yet when it grows, it is the largest of garden plants and becomes a tree, so that the birds of the air come and perch in its branches."
Matthew 13:31-32

17. Messiah, Your kingdom is like a mustard seed. How is it a mustard seed in me?

Date: ___/___/_____

_____
_____
_____
_____

He told them still another parable: "The kingdom of heaven is like yeast that a woman took and mixed into a large amount of flour until it worked all through the dough."
Matthew 13:33

18. Jesus, Your kingdom is like yeast. How is it like yeast in my city?

Date: ___/___/_____

_____
_____
_____
_____

"The kingdom of heaven is like treasure hidden in a field. When a man found it, he hid it again, and then in his joy went and sold all he had and bought that field.
Matthew 13:44

19. Lord, Your kingdom is a treasure. What do I treasure most?

Date: ___/___/_____

_____

_____

_____

_____

"Again, the kingdom of heaven is like a merchant looking for fine pearls. When he found one of great value, he went away and sold everything he had and bought it.
Matthew 13:45-46

20. Jesus, Your kingdom is like an expensive pearl. How can I buy this pearl?

Date: ___/___/_____

_____

_____

_____

_____

21. Christ, I want Your kingdom. Your kingdom is so valuable. How can I get Your kingdom?

Date: ___/___/_____

_____
_____
_____

"Once again, the kingdom of heaven is like a net that was let down into the lake and caught all kinds of fish.
Matthew 13:47

22. Jesus, Your kingdom is like a fishing net. What fish do You want me to catch?

Date: ___/___/_____

_____
_____
_____

When anyone hears the message about the kingdom and does not understand it, the evil one comes and snatches away what was sown in his heart.
This is the seed sown along the path.
Matthew 13:4,19

23. Dad, You want to soften my heart. What do you want to say?

Date: ___/___/_____

_____
_____
_____

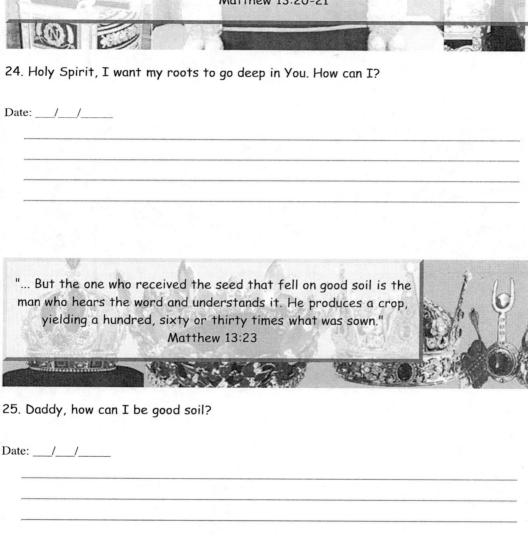

The one who received the seed that fell on rocky places is the man who hears the word and at once receives it with joy. But since he has no root, he lasts only a short time. When trouble or persecution comes because of the word, he quickly falls away.
Matthew 13:20-21

24. Holy Spirit, I want my roots to go deep in You. How can I?

Date: ___/___/_____

_____

_____

_____

_____

"... But the one who received the seed that fell on good soil is the man who hears the word and understands it. He produces a crop, yielding a hundred, sixty or thirty times what was sown."
Matthew 13:23

25. Daddy, how can I be good soil?

Date: ___/___/_____

_____

_____

_____

_____

26. Holy Spirit, I want to produce 100 times. How can I?

Date: ___/___/_____

_____

_____

_____

_____

For he must reign until he has put all his enemies under his feet. The last enemy to be destroyed is death.
1st Corinthians 15:25-26

27. Jesus, You gave me authority over death. Why? How can I use this authority?

Date: ___/___/_____

_____

_____

_____

_____

I will give you the keys of the kingdom of heaven;
whatever you bind on earth will be bound in heaven,
and whatever you loose on earth will be loosed in heaven."
Matthew 16:19

28. Messiah, You gave us the keys to the kingdom. How do You want me to use these keys?

Date: ___/___/_____

_____

_____

_____

_____

29. Christ, You already paid for sin and sickness on the cross. What do You want me to bind here?

Date: ___/___/_____

_____

_____

_____

_____

"I tell you the truth, whatever you bind on earth will be bound in heaven, and whatever you loose on earth will be loosed in heaven.
Matthew 18:18

30. Jesus, You want heaven to be loosed on earth. Right now, what do You want me to loose on earth?

Date: ___/___/_____

God's Goodness and Majesty

Totally Awesome!

Have you ever met a president or king—someone who is powerful? Were you a little nervous? God is more powerful than anyone else. He is the most awesome person. He is a King over all other kings. Thousands and thousands of angels bow down to Him. Angels and saints sing to Him all day and all night. He is totally perfect. God is brighter than the sun. He is so holy, that if we saw Him we would die. Today when people meet kings, they bow down and say, "Your Majesty." Jesus is our King. We bow down to Him.

Have you ever been around someone who became the leader—and then started acting mean? God is a powerful King. He can do anything He wants. But God is never mean. He is good all the time. He is so good, that He cannot do something bad. He never even thinks anything bad. It's amazing—He cannot be bad, because He is the source of all goodness. All bad things that happen do not come from His heart.

A father to the fatherless, a defender of widows, is God in his holy dwelling.
Psalm 68:5

1. Papa Father, I'm Your child. What do You feel about me?

Date: ___/___/_____

_____

_____

_____

_____

God sets the lonely in families, he leads forth the prisoners with singing; but the rebellious live in a sun-scorched land.
Psalm 68:6

2. Daddy, sometimes I feel lonely. What family are You setting me in? Why?

Date: ___/___/_____

_____

_____

_____

_____

> I will maintain my love to him forever,
> and my covenant with him will never fail.
> Psalm 89:28

3. Father You love me. You are always kind to me. Why do You covenant forever?

Date: ___/___/_____

_____

_____

_____

_____

> He who dwells in the shelter of the Most
> High will rest in the shadow of the Almighty.
> I will say of the Lord ,
> "He is my refuge and my fortress, my God,
> in whom I trust."
> Psalm 91:1-2

4. Papa, I'm totally safe in You. How can I rest in You more?

Date: ___/___/_____

_____

_____

_____

_____

You will not fear the terror of night,
nor the arrow that flies by day,
Psalm 91:5

5. Daddy, You don't want me to be afraid. Why do I not need to be afraid? What are You protecting me from?

Date: ___/___/_____

_____

_____

_____

_____

For he will command his angels concerning
you to guard you in all your ways;
they will lift you up in their hands,
so that you will not strike
your foot against a stone.
Psalm 91:11-12

6. Father, You told angels to protect me. Where are they? When do they help me?

Date: ___/___/_____

_____

_____

_____

_____

... proclaiming, "The Lord is upright; he is my Rock,
and there is no wickedness in him."
Psalm 92:15

7. Father God, You are my Rock. How are You completely good to me?

Date: ___/___/_____

_____

_____

_____

_____

The Lord reigns, he is robed in majesty;
the Lord is robed in majesty and is armed with strength.
The world is firmly established; it cannot be moved.
Psalm 93:1

8. Lord Jesus, You're clothed in majesty. What does that look like?

Date: ___/___/_____

_____

_____

_____

_____

Your statutes stand firm; holiness adorns
your house for endless days, O Lord .
Psalm 93:5

9. Jesus, I want to be like You. How can I be holy?

Date: ___/___/_____

_____

_____

_____

_____

10. Father, how does holiness adorn or clothe Your house? How can holiness adorn my house?

Date: ___/___/_____

_____

_____

_____

_____

In his hand are the depths of the earth,
and the mountain peaks belong to him.
The sea is his, for he made it,
and his hands formed the dry land.
Psalm 95:4-5

11. Lord, all the mountains, oceans, and land are Yours. How do You want me to use them?

Date: ___/___/_____

_____

_____

_____

... for he is our God and we are the people of his pasture,
the flock under his care.
Psalm 95:7

12. Papa, how am I a person of Your pasture?

Date: ___/___/_____

_____

_____

_____

13. Dad, how can I listen to Your voice better?

Date: ___/___/_____

_____

_____

_____

The King is mighty, he loves justice- you
have established equity; in Jacob you have
done what is just and right.
Psalm 99:4

14. Mighty King, You are just and fair. How can I be more just and fair?

Date: ___/___/_____

_____

_____

_____

_____

... who forgives all your sins and heals all your diseases...
Psalm 103:3

15. Jehovah-Raphe, Healer. What disease do You want me to heal today?

Date: ___/___/_____

_____

_____

_____

_____

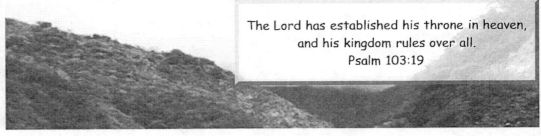

The Lord has established his throne in heaven,
and his kingdom rules over all.
Psalm 103:19

16. Dad, You rule over all the great leaders on earth. What kind of a King are You?

Date: ___/___/_____

_____

_____

_____

_____

Then they cried out to the Lord in their trouble,
and he delivered them from their distress.
Psalm 107:6

17. Daddy, why do You always answer me when I'm in trouble?

Date: ___/___/_____

_____

_____

_____

_____

Let them give thanks to the Lord for his unfailing
love and his wonderful deeds for men,
for he satisfies the thirsty and
fills the hungry with good things.
Psalm 107:8-9

18. Abba Papa, thank You. Why do You satisfy me and fill me? How?

Date: ___/___/_____

_____

_____

_____

For great is your love, higher than the heavens;
your faithfulness reaches to the skies.
Psalm 108:4

19. God, Your love never stops. It is higher than the stars. How can I know Your love more?

Date: ___/___/_____

_____

_____

_____

20. Abba Father, Your faithfulness to me is higher than the clouds. How have You been faithful to me?

Date: ___/___/_____

_____

_____

_____

Glorious and majestic are his deeds,
and his righteousness endures forever.
Psalm 111:3

21. Daddy, Your glory and majesty is amazing. What do You want to show me?

Date: ___/___/_____

_____

_____

_____

_____

He has caused his wonders to be remembered;
the Lord is gracious and compassionate.
Psalm 111:4

22. Papa Father, You have done wonders for me. Would You remind me of some of them?

Date: ___/___/_____

_____

_____

_____

_____

23. Father, You are gracious and compassionate to me. How can I be more like this?

Date: ___/___/_____

_____

_____

_____

_____

The highest heavens belong to the Lord ,
but the earth he has given to man.
Psalm 115:16

24. Lord, You have given the earth to all of us? What do You want me to do?

Date: ___/___/_____

_____

_____

_____

_____

Because he turned his ear to me,
I will call on him as long as I live.
Psalm 116:2

25. Papa, You watch the whole universe, yet You bend down and listen to me. Why listen to me?

Date: ___/___/_____

_____

_____

_____

_____

It is better to take refuge in the Lord than to trust in man.
Psalm 118:8

26. Dad, would You please show me how and when I trust in man?

Date: ___/___/_____

_____

_____

_____

_____

The Lord is my strength and my song;
he has become my salvation.
Psalm 118:14

27. Jesus, You're my Strength and Song. What are You singing right now?

Date: ___/___/_____

_____
_____
_____
_____

I will give you thanks, for you answered me;
you have become my salvation.
Psalm 118:21

28. Holy Spirit, what prayers did You answer?

Date: ___/___/_____

_____
_____
_____
_____

As the mountains surround Jerusalem, so the Lord surrounds his people both now and forevermore.
Psalm 125:2

29. Father, You surround and protect me. How?

Date: ___/___/_____

_____
_____
_____
_____

Sons are a heritage from the Lord , children a reward from him.
Psalm 127:3

30. Daddy, how am I a reward to my parents?

Date: ___/___/_____

_____
_____
_____
_____

The Attributes of God

Charater Counts

Did you ever mess up big time and knew you'd really be in trouble when someone found out? But then the most amazing thing happened! They forgave you and didn't ask you to pay for your mistake! That's mercy. You didn't get punished even though you deserved it. But what if right than, they gave you a huge gift? Grace is giving you a God given ability to do something you never could have done without His grace.

God is like that with us. He gives us mercy—over and over and over again. He forgives us for our sins every time we ask Him. He doesn't make us pay for our sin. No, He freely pardons the penalty we deserve for our sin. Why? Because Jesus paid that penalty when He died on the cross for us.

Not only that, God is constantly giving us grace. He is more gracious than any person who has ever lived. He never runs out of grace. Our Father is eagerly watching us. He is looking for ways to shower His love on us. He wants us to trust him and to freely receive all His good gifts to us. He does not want us to doubt that He is good. He does not want us to be afraid and wonder about bad things happening. He delights to give us everything good—not just what we need, but everything and anything that would be good for us, things way beyond what we could imagine.

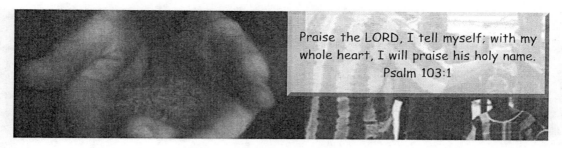

Praise the LORD, I tell myself; with my whole heart, I will praise his holy name.
Psalm 103:1

1. Jesus, I want to praise You with my whole soul. How can I?

Date: ___/___/_____

_____

_____

_____

_____

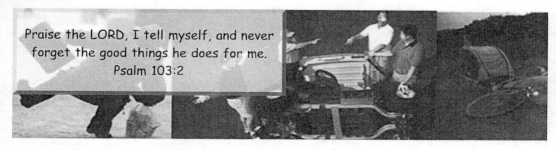

Praise the LORD, I tell myself, and never forget the good things he does for me.
Psalm 103:2

2. Father, You've done many good things for me. What good things have You done for me?

Date: ___/___/_____

_____

_____

_____

_____

He forgives all my sins and heals all my diseases.
Psalm 103:3

3. Messiah, You want to forgive ALL my sins. Why do You love me this much?

Date: ___/___/_____

_____

_____

_____

_____

4. Lord, why do You want to heal ALL my diseases? What do you want me to heal?

Date: ___/___/_____

_____

_____

_____

_____

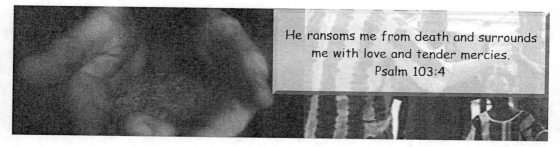

He ransoms me from death and surrounds
me with love and tender mercies.
Psalm 103:4

5. Jesus, You show me love and compassion. How?

Date: ___/___/_____

_____

_____

_____

_____

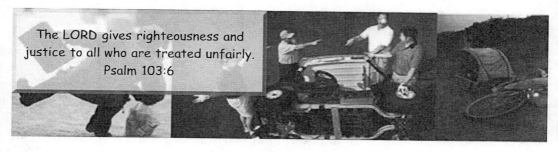

The LORD gives righteousness and
justice to all who are treated unfairly.
Psalm 103:6

6. Father, how can I help people who are treated unfairly. Who?

Date: ___/___/_____

_____

_____

_____

_____

He revealed his character to Moses and his deeds to the people of Israel.
Psalm 103:7

7. Dad, You showed your ways to Moses. How do You want to show me Your ways?

Date: ___/___/_____

_____

_____

_____

_____

The LORD is merciful and gracious; he is slow to get angry and full of unfailing love.
Psalm 103:8

8. Abba Father, You show love and patience. How do You show them to me?

Date: ___/___/_____

_____

_____

_____

_____

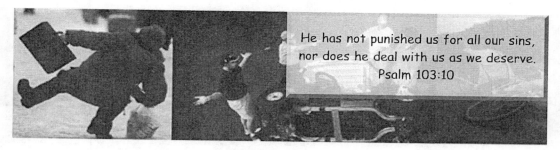

He has not punished us for all our sins,
nor does he deal with us as we deserve.
Psalm 103:10

9. Jesus, You don't punish me for my sins. Why not?

Date: ___/___/_____

_____

_____

_____

_____

For his unfailing love toward those who
fear him is as great as the height
of the heavens above the earth.
Psalm 103:11

10. Father, Wow! You are really great! How much do You love me?

Date: ___/___/_____

_____

_____

_____

_____

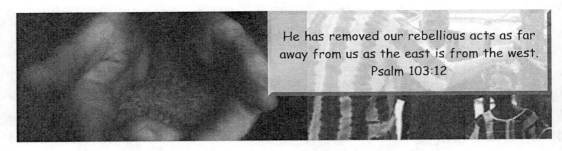

He has removed our rebellious acts as far away from us as the east is from the west.
Psalm 103:12

11. Dad, why are my sins this far away? How can I live believing this more?

Date: ___/___/_____

_____

_____

_____

_____

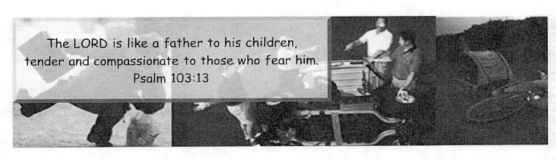

The LORD is like a father to his children, tender and compassionate to those who fear him.
Psalm 103:13

12. Father, How are You compassionate to me? Who can I be compassionate to?

Date: ___/___/_____

_____

_____

_____

_____

Our days on earth are like grass; like wildflowers,
we bloom and die. The wind blows,
and we are gone-- as though
we had never been here.
Psalm 103:15-16

13. Dad, our lives are so short. How can I use my time well?

Date: ___/___/_____

_____

_____

_____

_____

But the love of the LORD remains forever
with those who fear him. His salvation
extends to the children's children
Psalm 103:17

14. Lord, Your love remains forever. Why forever?

Date: ___/___/_____

_____

_____

_____

_____

The LORD has made the heavens his throne;
from there he rules over everything.
Psalm 103:19

15. Abba Father, heaven is Your throne. How can I extend Your rule on earth?

Date: ___/___/_____

_____

_____

_____

_____

Praise the LORD, you angels of his,
you mighty creatures who carry out his plans,
listening for each of his commands.
Psalm 103:20

16. Jesus, angels are mighty and often visited people. How can I listen to Your commands more?

Date: ___/___/_____

_____

_____

_____

_____

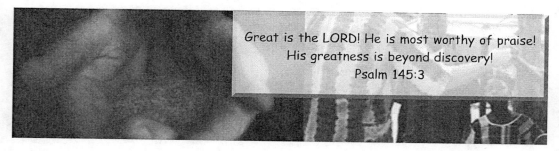

Great is the LORD! He is most worthy of praise!
His greatness is beyond discovery!
Psalm 145:3

17. Father, How can I discover more of your greatness?

Date: ___/___/_____

_____
_____
_____
_____

Everyone will share the story of your
wonderful goodness; they will sing
with joy of your righteousness.
Psalm 145:7

18. Dad, You are so good and joyful. Why? How can I be more joyful?

Date: ___/___/_____

_____
_____
_____
_____

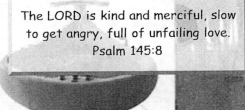

The LORD is kind and merciful, slow to get angry, full of unfailing love.
Psalm 145:8

19. Jesus, how are You rich in love to me?

Date: ___/___/_____

_____

_____

_____

_____

All of your works will thank you, LORD, and your faithful followers will bless you.
Psalm 145:10

20. Lord, how does ALL You've made praise You? How can I be more faithful?

Date: ___/___/_____

_____

_____

_____

_____

They will talk together about the glory of your kingdom; they will celebrate examples of your power.
Psalm 145:11

21. Jesus, how can I talk of Your power?

Date: ___/___/_____

_____

_____

_____

_____

They will tell about your mighty deeds and about the majesty and glory of your reign.
Psalm 145:12

22. King Jesus, the majesty and glory of Your reign is awesome! How do You want to show me Yourself?

Date: ___/___/_____

_____

_____

_____

_____

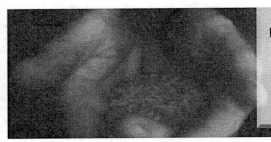

For your kingdom is an everlasting kingdom.
You rule generation after generation.
The LORD is faithful in all he says;
he is gracious in all he does.
Psalm 145:13

23. Jesus, why is Your kingdom everlasting?

Date: ___/___/_____

_____
_____
_____
_____

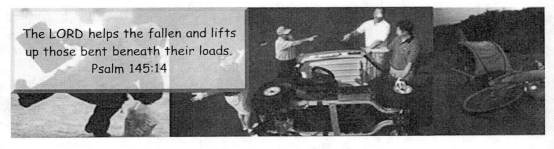

The LORD helps the fallen and lifts
up those bent beneath their loads.
Psalm 145:14

24. Father, all Your promises will come true. What have You promised me?

Date: ___/___/_____

_____
_____
_____
_____

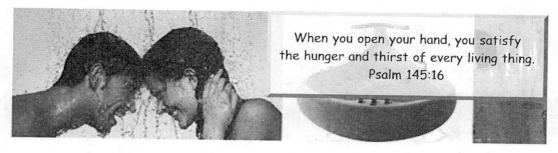

When you open your hand, you satisfy the hunger and thirst of every living thing.
Psalm 145:16

25. Abba Daddy, some people are poor and hungry. How can I help them? Who?

Date: ___/___/_____

_____

_____

_____

_____

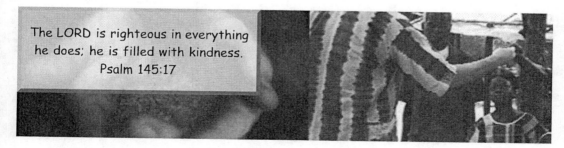

The LORD is righteous in everything he does; he is filled with kindness.
Psalm 145:17

26. Lord, You are filled with love. How can I be loving like You?

Date: ___/___/_____

_____

_____

_____

_____

The LORD is close to all who call on him,
yes, to all who call on him sincerely.
Psalm 145:18

27. Papa, You listen when I talk to You. How are You near to me?

Date: ___/___/_____

_____

_____

_____

_____

He fulfills the desires of those who fear him;
he hears their cries for help and rescues them.
Psalm 145:19

28. Father, why do You fulfill my desires?

Date: ___/___/_____

_____

_____

_____

_____

29. Daddy, You always hear me. How do You save me?

Date: ___/___/_____

_____

_____

_____

_____

The LORD protects all those who love him,
but he destroys the wicked.

Psalm 145:20

30. Father, how do You protect me?

Date: ___/___/_____

_____

_____

_____

_____